David Douglas Bannerman

The Worship of the Presbyterian Church

With Special Reference to the Question of Liturgies

David Douglas Bannerman

The Worship of the Presbyterian Church
With Special Reference to the Question of Liturgies

ISBN/EAN: 9783337293048

Printed in Europe, USA, Canada, Australia, Japan

Cover: Foto ©Lupo / pixelio.de

More available books at **www.hansebooks.com**

THE WORSHIP

OF

THE PRESBYTERIAN CHURCH,

WITH SPECIAL REFERENCE TO

THE QUESTION OF LITURGIES.

BY

REV. D. D. BANNERMAN, M.A.,

AUTHOR OF "GROUNDS AND METHODS OF ADMISSION TO
SEALING ORDINANCES."

Edinburgh:
ANDREW ELLIOT, 17 PRINCES STREET.
1884.

PREFATORY NOTE.

In the Spring of last year I had occasion to write a Paper for the Perth Theological Society, on "The Place and Use of a Liturgy or Book of Common Order in a Presbyterian Church." This was read at a meeting of the Society on 18th June, 1883. Shortly afterwards I was asked to give an Address at a Provincial Church Congress, to be held in Glasgow in November, under the auspices of the Free Church Synod of Glasgow and Ayr; the topic prescribed by the Programme Committee being "The Ideal of Presbyterian Worship."

What is now printed is, with some additions, what was given in those two Papers. It is published as a contribution to the discussion of an important subject, which has been awakening considerable interest of late in several branches of the Presbyterian Church on both sides of the Atlantic.

D. D. B.

St. Leonard's, Perth,
February, 1884.

CONTENTS.

CHAPTER I.

THE IDEAL OF PRESBYTERIAN WORSHIP.

PAGE

(1.) Spiritual—Conscious and intelligent participation by worshippers—"What is prayer?" 1-3

(2.) Scriptural—Scripture rule of worship from standpoint of Reformed or Calvinistic Church, as compared with Lutheran and Anglican—No new element—New Testament canons for worship as to its circumstances and arrangements—Westminster Confession—Illustration in case of instrumental music, ... 4-6

(3.) The Word of God central in worship—"Lecturing"—Dignity and seemliness of service—First Book of Discipline, ... 6-8

(4.) Congregational—All to join—Individuality to be developed in *congregation* as a whole, as well as in members separately—"Uniformity and purity of worship"—Different "environment," 9-12

(5.) Simple and elastic—Capacity of adaptation to circumstances and emergencies, ... 12f.

CHAPTER II.

DUTY OF THE CHURCH AS SUCH IN REFERENCE TO THE ORDER AND FORMS OF WORSHIP—LITURGIES.

A "liturgy" may be opposed or approved according to definition—Use of term in Scripture; in Primitive Church. Dr. Bannerman's definition—Such liturgies to be always opposed, ... 14-16

PAGE

Heads of argument against liturgies of Anglican type—Scripture principles and example—Nature and constitution of Church of Christ—Spirit of Gospel dispensation, . 17-19

Early Christian worship—Justin Martyr's account—Free prayer and "Amen" said by people, ... 19-21

Psalms and hymns in early Church—Growth of liturgies, ... 21-24

Practical evils arising from fixed liturgies—Illustrations—Dr. Phillips Brooks—Prof. Lorimer of Edinburgh—Siege of Paris—Funeral service of Church of England, . .24-9

CHAPTER III.

THEORY AND PRACTICE OF SCOTTISH CHURCH AS TO PUBLIC WORSHIP; THE SCOTTISH METRICAL PSALMS; WESTMINSTER DIRECTORY FOR WORSHIP.

Ought the Reformed Church to leave everything free as regards order and forms of worship?—Answer given by Scottish Church and others—Advantages of such a system—Spiritual life and spiritual sympathy, ...30-3

Psalmody at the Reformation—The Scottish Metrical Psalter: its authors and history—Characteristics and associations—Forms a national liturgy of praise and prayer—The "Paraphrases," 34-40

Westminster Directory: its merits; much of it practically in abeyance; revision called for—Unwritten tradition of Scottish worship, ... 40-43

This state of things greatly preferable to a fixed and invariable liturgy; but is there a middle ground? . .43f.

CHAPTER IV.

LITURGIES OR BOOKS OF COMMON ORDER AS USED BY THE MAJORITY OF THE REFORMED CHURCHES; DANGERS AND ADVANTAGES.

An optional liturgy, a lawful arrangement for the "seemly form and order" of public worship in Presby-

CONTENTS.

	PAGE
terian Church—In use in Scottish Church till Westminster Assembly—Why given up then, ...	45-7
Edwards on Lawfulness of set forms of prayers—Dr. John Duncan—Dr. Chalmers, ...	48f.
Assuming the lawfulness of an optional liturgy, what is to be said of it on grounds of expediency, ...	49

Objection first: "Un-Presbyterian; Covenanters against liturgies"—Answer: Historically incorrect—Jenny Geddes—Facts of the case—Absence of read prayers, one of the grievances of the Covenanters—Dickson of Irvine on the old liturgy and the new—Prelates condemned for "interdicting morning and evening prayers"—Alexander Henderson at Glasgow Assembly, ... 49-55

Objection second: "Wrong tendency—Externalism—Practically playing into hands of Prelatists," . . . 56

Answer: Dangers admitted; but hold chiefly in case of fixed and enforced liturgy—Historic position of Reformed Church in Scotland and elsewhere in this matter—Alexander Henderson as representative and exponent of it—His criticism of Laud's liturgy—His opposition to views and practices of English sectaries in worship—Controversy on subject—"Discountenancing read prayers"—Conference on innovations in Lord Loudon's chambers—Robert Baillie's troubles at Kilwinning—Henderson's statement for Westminster Assembly, ... 56-63

Scottish Collects of 1595—Alexander Henderson's opinion of the prayers of old Scottish liturgy—Mr. Gladstone on Scottish worship, ... 64-6

Objection third: "Practically hurtful—Liturgy and free prayer cannot live together—Staff will be made a crutch" 67f.

Answer: Risks admitted—Argument conclusive against liturgy of Anglican type, but not against historic position of Reformed Church — Individual "offices"—Evidence of experience—Nature of Knox's liturgy—Its rubrics—Practical results in Church—Robert Bruce in Edinburgh and Inverness—Alexander Henderson in Glasgow Assembly—Moravian Brethren—Dutch Reformed Church, . 69-75

	PAGE

Advantages of such an optional liturgy in way of help, stimulus, and guidance—People's share in worship—The Lord's Prayer and the "Amen"—Use of Apostle's Creed in old Scottish Church—Service-book for special occasions—"Rights of Christian people" in baptism and marriage, . 76-9

Early Christian liturgies and those of Reformation period—The Reformation "Confession of Sins" of 1525—The Communion of Saints, ... 79-82

APPENDICES.

APPENDIX A.—JOHN KNOX'S USE OF APOSTLES' CREED AND PRAYERS OF BOOK OF COMMON ORDER IN HIS LAST ILLNESS, ... 83-8

The "prayer for the sick" and "evening prayer," . 88-90

APPENDIX B.—SCOTTISH COLLECTS OF 1595—History and Characteristics—Thomas Bassandyne before Assembly of 1568—Scottish Words 91-4

I. Prayers relating to individual Christian life and experience, ... 94-101
II. Prayers for blessing in use of means of grace, . 101-104
III. Prayers for the Church, ... 105-109
IV. Prayers for the nation and its rulers, ... 109
V. Prayers bearing on a Christian's relations to other men, ... 109-112
VI. Thanksgiving and Praise to God, . . . 112f.

APPENDIX C.—THE REFORMATION CONFESSION OF SINS, 1525—History—Confession of Sin in Anglican Prayer-Book—German Text—French Versions, . . 113-118

THE WORSHIP

OF

THE PRESBYTERIAN CHURCH.

CHAPTER I.

THE IDEAL OF PRESBYTERIAN WORSHIP.

WHAT is the ideal of Presbyterian worship? Without pretending to give a complete answer, or to divide it in a perfectly logical way, I think that the following points enter into the ideal of worship, as regarded from the standpoint of the Presbyterian or Reformed Church [1]:—

I. The worship must be Spiritual; and
II. It must be Scriptural.

The whole ideal might be described under these two heads. But where those two great

---

[1] I use the word "Reformed" here in the sense in which it is universally employed on the Continent,—namely, to denote the Churches whose Confessions of Faith are of the Calvinistic, as distinguished from the Lutheran type.

conditions are observed, certain other features become practically so outstanding as to deserve separate notice.

III. The Word of God, by which the worship is moulded, has the central place in it.

IV. The worship is Congregational; and

V. It is simple and elastic.

I. The Worship must be Spiritual.

The whole question of worship is ruled by that saying of our Lord's, which often meets one in such a striking way amid the corruptions of Romanism in Italy, written in clear letters over the door of some Waldensian mission Church: "God is a Spirit; and they that worship Him must worship Him in spirit and in truth."[1]

We worship God when we hold such fellowship with Him as "the Father of our spirits," "the God and Father of our Lord Jesus Christ;" He speaking to us, and we to Him. The first essential condition of private or public worship, from the standpoint of the Church of the Reformation, is that it be not a form merely, but a reality,—that there be a conscious intelligent forthgoing of the spirit of the worshipper to God in all the parts of the service. "Prayer," as the first clause of that familiar answer in the Cate-

---

[1] John iv. 24; comp. Phil. iii. 3.

chism puts it, "is an offering up of *our desires* unto God."[1] If the things said are not *our* desires, it is not prayer at all so far as we are concerned.

This principle has many applications; but these are so obvious that I omit them, and pass on to the second condition of worship, from the standpoint of the Reformed Church :—

II. It must be Scriptural.

By this I mean, with respect to the *substance* of the worship, that it must be offered to God as revealed in His Word; and, with respect to the *form* of it—with which we have more especially to do here—that the worship, as to its elements, must be authorised by Scripture; and, as to the adjustment of those elements, must be in accordance with the two great Scriptural canons for New Testament worship, "Let all things be done unto edification"; and "Let all things be done in good (or seemly) form, and according to order."[2]

---

[1] "Prayer is an offering up of our desires unto God for things agreeable to His will, in the name of Christ, with confession of our sins, and thankful acknowledgment of His mercies."—*Shorter Catechism*, ques. 98.

[2] Πάντα πρὸς οἰκοδομὴν γενέσθω. Πάντα εὐσχημόνως καὶ κατὰ τάξιν γενέσθω.—1 Cor. xiv. 26, 40. Ἐυσχημόνως in classic Greek is commonly used in reference to personal demeanour and bearing. It may often be translated, "with dignity," "like a gentleman."

Scripture, as it is read in the Reformed or Calvinistic Church, "forbids the worshipping of God by images, or in any other way not appointed in His Word."[1] We are bound to produce distinct Scriptural authority "for every substantial element or feature of our religious services."

Now, I believe this Calvinistic principle of Church worship, as distinguished from the Lutheran or Anglican one,—which claims power for the Church to introduce rites and ceremonies in the worship of God, if only they are not expressly *forbidden* in Scripture, — to be thoroughly sound and of much practical importance, provided always that it be taken with the necessary limitation so clearly stated in the Westminster Confession, that "there are *some circumstances* concerning the worship of God and government of the Church common to human actions and societies, which are to be ordered by the light of nature and Christian prudence" (*i.e.*, Christian common-sense), "according to the general rules of the Word, which are always to be observed."[2] It is good that each proposal

---

[1] *Shorter Catechism*, ques. 51.

[2] Conf. i. 6.—Thus, for instance, instrumental music, as an accompaniment to the voice, is a "circumstance common to the human action" of singing among all nations. It occurs as such in connection with singing to the praise of God in Bible history, altogether apart from the Tabernacle or Temple service—as, for example, in the case of Miriam and the Israelites at the Red

for change in worship should be challenged by this warder at the door of the Church, and should have to give a strict account of itself, and even of its parentage and connections. If what is proposed prove to be really a new element in worship, a new way of worshipping God by man's device, let it be kept out by all means. If, on the other hand, it prove to be simply a circumstantial variation, a new arrangement for

Sea (Exod. xv.). Therefore, instrumental music, if kept strictly in a subordinate place, as a mere aid and accompaniment to the voice, may be fairly held to be in accordance with the Calvinistic rule for worship.

In point of fact, this has been the conclusion of almost every Presbyterian Church which has had to face the question of instrumental aid to praise, separately and on its own merits. Previous to the Reformation, instrumental music had been grossly abused in the Church of Rome. It had been one of the chief means of silencing the voice of the people in the House of God altogether. No one can wonder, therefore, that the Reformers in some countries were disposed to sweep it away *en masse* with other flagrant abuses in worship with which it was associated. They did so, undoubtedly, in some cases, by bringing it somewhat hastily under the Calvinistic principle of Church worship above stated. But it is worth noting how, with hardly a single exception, every Reformed Church in Britain, America, or the Continent of Europe, which in calmer times has had to consider the subject of instrumental music in worship, has come deliberately to the same conclusion—namely, that while all due regard should be paid in such matters to the peace of congregations and the associations of devout worshippers, there is nothing either in the Word of God or in the principles and constitution of the Presbyterian Church, to preclude the use of instrumental music in public worship as an aid to vocal praise.

the seemly and profitable use of an old ordinance, let it be admitted, where that is for edification; but let it be kept carefully in the subordinate place to which alone it has a right by its own account of itself in asking admission.[1]

Here again one is tempted to enlarge and illustrate; but I pass to the third characteristic of Presbyterian worship, which emerges wherever the two great conditions already named are at all realised in practice.

III. THE WORD OF GOD, BY WHICH THE WORSHIP IS MOULDED, HAS THE CENTRAL PLACE IN IT.

God, speaking to men in the Scriptures, has called them into fellowship with Himself in Jesus Christ and with each other in His Church. We meet together in God's house, not only for common praise and prayer, but very specially that we may hear Him speaking further to us, opening to us the Scriptures by His Spirit through His ordinance of the ministry. He has many things to say, and we are dull of hearing.

---

[1] This point is well put in a report on instrumental music submitted to last General Assembly of the Free Church of Scotland (see "Blue Book, 1883," Append. xxxvii. p. 26). For a thorough discussion of the whole subject of the extent and limits of Church power in reference to public worship, see the chapter on "Rites and Ceremonies" in Dr. Bannerman's work, *The Church of Christ*, i. 335-75.

And we need ever afresh to be "stirred up by being put in remembrance."

The strength of the Presbyterian service, as almost all admit, has lain here: in its practical carrying out of the great Reformation principle of the supremacy of Scripture; in its direct appeal at once to the intellect, the heart, and the conscience, through the reading and preaching of the Word of God as such. I do not dwell on this characteristic just because it is so unmistakable. Two things only I wish to say before passing on:

1st. The method of "lecturing" or expository preaching, which has always been in special favour with the Scottish Church in her best days, is of the highest value in this connection, inasmuch as, if conscientiously and intelligently used, it secures, as nothing else can, variety and freshness. It makes both the preacher and his hearers feel that the Book of Revelation, like the Book of Nature, is *Divine*, because it is inexhaustible.

2nd. The belief in the supremacy and divinity of Scripture, wherever that belief has been a living thing in the Reformed Church, has done much to secure the essential dignity and seemliness of the whole service. It has done so in Scotland, wherever the spirit of our first Reformers has prevailed. There are several striking passages in the "First Book of Discipline" which bring this out. The book was drawn up in 1560, by Knox, Willock, Row, and other leading men. In speaking, for instance, of the due repair of the parish Churches, they say: "Lest that the Word of God and ministration of the Sacraments *by unseemliness of the place* come in contempt, of necessity it is that the Kirk and place where the people ought publicly to convene be with expedition repaired, . . . and have such preparation within as appertaineth as well to *the majesty of the Word of God*, as unto the ease and commodity of the people." "We desire," they say again, "that burial (*i.e.*, the actual interment of the dead) be so honourably handled that the hope of our resurrection may be nourished. . . . Burial should be without the Kirk in a fine air, and the place walled and keepit honourably."[1]

It is not on John Knox nor on the Fathers of the Scottish Church that the blame should be laid for barn-like Churches, irreverent funerals, or ill-kept churchyards in Scotland. The Moderatism of the eighteenth century and the meanness of heritors trained and influenced by Moderatism, have had much more to do with the matter.

---

[1] Dunlop, *Collection of Confessions*, vol. ii. 598, 623.

IV. The Worship must be Congregational.

By this I mean two things. First, that all the congregation must join in all the parts of the service, ὅση δύναμις αὐτοῖς—to use a phrase of Justin Martyr's—" according to their ability." This is certainly a point on which, as I may show presently, Presbyterian worship in the concrete is open to just criticism. But as certainly it belongs to the ideal of worship from the standpoint of the Presbyterian Church.

But, secondly, I mean that the worship of each particular congregation ought to be worthy of that congregation as a whole in view of its special history, character, and gifts. The true genius of Presbyterianism aims at the natural and wholesome development of *individuality* within due limits in the congregation, as well as in each Christian man and woman who is a member therein.

Our elders in Scotland promise, in accordance with Act 11 of Assembly 1700, to "observe uniformity of worship and of the administration of all public ordinances within this Church, as the same are at present performed and allowed." The formula for ministers, which dates from 1711, is in this respect more general in its terms, as if a somewhat wider discretion, as to details of worship, were left with them. They "own the purity of worship presently authorised and practised in this Church . . . as founded on the Word of God and agreeable thereto;" and they "promise that in their practice they will conform themselves to the said worship, . . . and follow no divisive courses therefrom."[1] Neither ministers nor elders promise to observe identity in the details of worship. And a very interesting variety in "the administration of public ordinances," within certain limits, has always prevailed and been "allowed in this Church." What our ministers are bound to is, that they conform themselves as regards the public services of God's house to the well-known type of Presbyterian worship founded on the great Scriptural principle concerning purity of worship, as held by the Reformed Church, with its equally Scriptural canon of interpretation as to the "circumstances of worship."[2]

The individuality of a congregation in a purely mining district is quite distinct from that of a congregation in a pastoral one; and both of these, again, are very different in history and character from a congregation in a fishing village,

---

[1] See "Report of Scottish Sub-Committee on Creeds and Formulas of Subscription to General Presbyterian Council at Philadelphia in 1880," in "Proceedings of Council," 973 f., 987 f. Comp. "Act anent Questions and Formula, 1846, xii." in "Free Church Standards."

[2] Comp. "Report on Instrumental Music," *ut supra*, p. 6.

or from a West-end city charge. Given an equally high spiritual condition in all the four cases, the congregational individuality will and should develop itself differently in worship in each of them respectively.

It will be objected, perhaps: "This is making class distinctions where none ought to be admitted." But the answer is very plain. It is not *making* distinctions. It is simply recognising facts in Providence, which are *there*, whether you recognise them or not, and seeking to act accordingly. In what is highest and deepest in their worship, in the great essentials of it, all Christian congregations, worshipping in a spiritual and Scriptural way, are one, and rejoice to know and feel that they are so. But, in the circumstantials of their worship, there may be, and there ought to be, a good deal of difference.

The whole "environment" of the members of a West-end congregation in Edinburgh or Glasgow is, by necessity of nature, very different from that of a congregation amid the mining "rows" of Ayrshire or the Lothians, or in the Highlands of the north or of the south of Scotland. No slight to the one nor exaltation of the other, in a moral or spiritual point of view, is at all implied in our recognising that fact. The members of the city congregation and of the country one live in different sorts of houses; they hear and join in a different kind of music during the week. If they are to be *themselves* on the Lord's Day, it follows that the house which they rear for the worship of God, and the form in which they praise Him there will, in some respects, be different also. What would be most creditable to the one congregation, and would justly command the respect and touch the heart of the most intelligent and cultured stranger worshipping with them, would be most unworthy of the other. It would have quite a different aspect and meaning there.

V. The Worship must be Simple and Elastic.

This follows necessarily from what has already been said. If the worship is to be congregational, it must, speaking generally, be strictly simple. The spirit of Presbyterianism demands that, above all, the common man[1] shall have his full place in the worship of the congregation—not as a concession, but as of right. With all due care, therefore, for the dignity and good taste of the service—which are perfectly compatible with its simplicity,—it must not, in prayer or praise, go

---

[1] I borrow a phrase from a fine passage on what is meant by Presbyterianism, in Principal Rainy's "Three Lectures on the Church of Scotland," ed. 1883, p. 36.

beyond what may be fairly asked of an ordinary, earnest, and intelligent member of the Church.

And the service must be elastic enough to meet all the emergencies of life for the individual, the congregation, and the Church at large. It must be able to adapt itself to the need of the humblest, and to command the respect and interest of the most cultured. It must suit the case of every company of worshippers by sea and land, in the city and the wilderness, in time of war and time of peace.

So much for the ideal roughly sketched. In the following chapters I propose to say something as to the practical steps which the Church as such may and should take to secure these ends.

CHAPTER II.

DUTY OF THE CHURCH AS SUCH IN REFERENCE TO THE ORDER AND FORMS OF WORSHIP: LITURGIES.

IN considering this subject, it is of special importance to define our terms. From the standpoint of the Presbyterian or Reformed Church, a "liturgy" may be either opposed or approved, according to what you understand by it. The word "liturgy" ($\lambda\epsilon\iota\tau o\upsilon\rho\gamma\acute{\iota}a$) is a Scriptural one, occurring six times as a substantive in the New Testament. It is always used there to denote the worship or service of God, and is rendered in our English Version "ministration," "ministry," or more often "service."[1] By an easy transition, it came afterwards to mean the order of Divine service, or the form of words used in worship.

There were two parts of the worship of the primitive Church which naturally tended to assume a more or less fixed shape before the

---

[1] Luke i. 23; 2 Cor. ix. 12; Phil. ii. 17, 30; Heb. viii. 6, 9, 21.

rest. These were the two Sacraments of Christ's appointment. On the one hand, what is usually known as the "Apostles' Creed" grew by degrees out of Baptism in the name of the Trinity, with the corresponding confession of faith made by converts from heathenism; and on the other, the Communion Service in the different Churches crystallised naturally into a regular form round our Lord's words of institution. "The liturgy," in the early centuries, meant the order of Communion. It is in this sense that the word is used when we speak of "the liturgy of Jerusalem" (or "of St. James"), "the liturgy of Alexandria" (or "of St. Mark"), &c. It is of these in their original forms that President Hitchcock says truly: "At first the liturgies were oral, flexible, and varied. Not till after the Nicene epoch were they reduced to writing. Later still was the Roman usurpation with intolerance and exclusion of other forms."[1]

Popularly, the word "liturgy" has now come to mean a prescribed form of words for all the parts of public worship, a fixed ritual like that of the Church of England or the Church of Rome. That is probably what is conveyed to the minds of most people in Scotland when any one speaks of a liturgy. Some writers, again—as, for instance, Dr. R. M. Patterson, in an able

[1] *Proceedings of Council at Philadelphia*, p. 74.

article on "Presbyterian Worship" lately published [1]—use the term liturgy in a somewhat arbitrary and restricted sense, to denote a service in which responsive prayers and readings of Scripture form the main feature. That, of course, is not what is meant by such authors as the late Mr. Baird, or Dr. Charles Hodge in writing on the subject of "Presbyterian Liturgies"; nor by President Hitchcock when he says that "the Directory of Worship set forth by the Westminster Assembly concedes the liturgical idea." [2]

Dr. Bannerman, in his comprehensive treatise on the Church, lays down three marks of the kind of liturgy which he opposes. First, it involves a scheme of fixed forms for the *ordinary* worship of the Church *at all times*. Secondly, these are used *alone*, to the absolute exclusion of the possibility of free prayer. Thirdly, the use of these forms is made *compulsory* by ecclesiastical authority.[3] It was a liturgy of that kind, with equally objectionable accompaniments, which Charles I. and Archbishop Laud tried to force upon the Church of Scotland in 1637, with what results all the world knows. Practically, it is a liturgy of that type which we see at present established in the Episcopal Church of England,

---

[1] *Presbyterian Review*, Oct. 1883, p. 745.
[2] *Proceedings of Council at Philadelphia*, p. 74.
[3] *Church of Christ*, i. 383.

and in the Scottish Episcopal Church. Such a liturgy must always meet with unanimous opposition from all true Presbyterians. No plea of beauty and impressiveness as to the words employed, nor venerable associations as to their origin and ancient use, can ever justify a form of service involving the three elements above stated.

It is hardly needful to bring forward in detail the arguments which prove the unlawfulness of such a liturgy. They are to be drawn from the general principles of God's Word bearing upon the subject of worship, from the example of our Lord and his Apostles, from the nature and constitution of the Church of Christ, and the rights and liberties of her members,—from the whole spirit and character of the Gospel dispensation.[1]

The essentially free and spiritual character of the true worship of God plainly forbids any such use of prescribed formulæ in prayer as would exclude or even discourage the natural utterance of the heart according to the varying circumstances of the believing man, the believing family, and the believing congregation. If they are to pray to God "*e corde*" and "*ex animo*," they must often pray in the fullest sense "*ex tempore*," according to the *time* and the situation

---

[1] Bannerman, *Church of Christ*, i. 385-91; with the full references given there to the literature of this subject.

in which they now find themselves under His providence. No prayer-book, however excellent and comprehensive, can possibly make provision for this. No Christian minister and congregation who have felt in their own experience how the free Spirit of God, "the Spirit of grace and supplications," "the Lord and Giver of life," meets the necessities of such an hour by His inspiring and suggesting influences, will ever consent to forego a privilege so great and precious.

No one, again, who candidly studies the teaching of Scripture on this subject can fail to recognise the place and honour which it gives to free prayer; nor can they, in the light of that teaching, approve of any liturgical arrangement which would tend to shut it out from the public services of God's house. For the Church, by any such arrangement, to hinder or discourage her ministers from acquiring and improving the gift and grace of free prayer, is to undertake a very grave responsibility. To bind the consciences of her ministers and members in all the public services to certain set forms of prayer, is a serious interference with the liberty wherewith Christ has made His people free.

We find no Scripture evidence whatever that fixed and invariable forms of prayer were used either in the Old Testament Church or in the New. There is, on the other hand, very clear

Scripture evidence that free prayer was used in the public worship of the Church under both dispensations.[1] The same thing holds, both negatively and positively, of the worship of the post-Apostolic Church in the first three or four centuries.

In Justin Martyr's interesting account of the simple worship of the Christians of the first half of the second century nothing is more obvious than that with them prayer was free. "There is then brought to the president of the brethren," he says, in describing the administration of the Lord's Supper, "bread and a cup of wine mixed with water. And he, taking them, gives praise and glory to the Father of the universe through the name of the Son and of the Holy Ghost, and offers thanks at considerable length for our being counted worthy to receive these things at His hands. And when he has concluded the prayers and thanksgivings, all the people express their assent by saying 'Amen.' This word 'Amen' answers in the Hebrew language to 'So be it.' And when the president has given thanks, and all the people have expressed their assent, those who are called by us deacons give to each of those present to partake of the bread and wine mixed with water, over which the thanksgiving was pro-

---

[1] Comp. Bannerman, *ut supra*, 386-88; M'Crie, *Review of Simeon on the English Liturgy* in *Miscellaneous Works*, 210-14; Robinson, *Case of Liturgies*, 49-76.

nounced." In a subsequent chapter Justin says : "On the day called Sunday, all who live in cities or in the country gather together to one place, and the memoirs of the apostles, or the writings of the prophets, are read as long as time permits. Then we all rise together and pray ; and as we before said, when our prayer is ended, bread and wine and water are brought, and the president in like manner offers prayers and thanksgivings, according to his ability (ὅση δύναμις αὐτῷ), and the people assent, saying 'Amen.'"[1] It might

---

[1] Justin Martyr, *Apol.* i. 65, 67. I quote from Dr. Marcus Dods' translation in the "Ante-Nicene Library," edited by Dr. Roberts and Professor Donaldson, ii. 63-65. The undeniable presence of free prayer—and that at the Communion service—in this first picture of Christian worship drawn by a Christian hand in the sub-Apostolic Church, has given a good deal of trouble to some advocates of fixed liturgies. "The words, 'as well as he is able'" Principal Daniel reluctantly admits, "would seem to imply that some portions of the service at least were extemporised; but, even if such were the case, this liberty was unquestionably very soon taken away." *The Prayer-Book*, 8th ed. p. 7. One would be glad to know when and by what authority "this liberty was taken away" from the Church. Certainly Tertullian, at the end of the second century, or the beginning of the third, knew nothing of such a change when he said, speaking of the public worship of Christians : "We pray without a monitor, because we pray from the heart," *Apol.* 30. "Whatever part of the Christian service this may refer to," says Dr. Jacob, "*Sine monitore quia de pectore oramus,* must mean extemporaneous prayer," *Eccles. Polity of New Testament*, p. 222. For a very able and fair discussion by an Episcopalian writer of the question of the practice of the early Church in this matter, see the whole section, pp. 215-29.

be well if all the members of our congregations did their part in that respect still, as the presidents seek to do theirs, ὅση δύναμις αὐτοῖς, "to the best of their ability."

As has been already pointed out, forms of prayer and orders of service naturally grew up by degrees in various Christian communities for such parts of worship as Baptism and the Lord's Supper. The materials both for praise and prayer multiplied as the spiritual life and gifts of the office-bearers and members of the Church were developed and bore fruit.

Throughout the Roman Empire, Christian congregations sprang, as a rule, out of the Jewish synagogues. The Psalms were, therefore, naturally the first, and for a time almost the only materials of praise. Besides what followed from their place in inspired Scripture, they embodied for the Hebrew Christian the hallowed memories of more than a thousand years. For Christians both of Jewish and Gentile origin they represented and embodied in a living and practical way the great truth that God's believing people, under all changes of dispensation, are essentially one in all that is deepest and highest in their spiritual experience. The Psalms, to the early Christians, formed an unbroken link between "the Church in the wilderness," the Church militant under the Gospel, and the Church of the redeemed above. In them, as in the praises of heaven heard by the Apostle in his vision in Patmos, "the song of Moses, the servant of God," was joined with "the song of the Lamb."[1] It is true, indeed, that the first mention of praise in Christian worship, beyond the pages of the New Testament, is of "a hymn to Christ as God."[2] The "Gloria in Excelsis" and the "Ter Sanctus" occur in some of the oldest known liturgies; and the "Te Deum" in its earliest forms follows not long after.[3] But such noble Christian hymns as these had to be made before they could be sung; and it was not in every generation that Christian singers capable of making them were raised up. Such hymns had to approve themselves to the judgment and heart of the Church, as worthy of a place in public worship, before they could be generally received and used. This did not take

---

[1] Rev. xv. 3.

[2] In the well-known letter of Pliny to Trajan, written in the first decade of the second century. Justin Martyr also in speaking of Christian worship (circa 140 A.D.) says, "We offer thanks to the Maker of the universe by solemn invocations and hymns" (διὰ λόγου πομπὰς καὶ ὕμνους πέμπομεν) *Apol.* i. 13. But these "hymns to the Maker of the universe," may have been like that which our Lord and His disciples sang together before going out to Gethsemane (Matt. xxvi. 30), which was in all likelihood one of the *Paschal Psalms*, or *Hallel*, Ps. cxiii.-cxviii. The word "hymn" in the early Christian Church was often used of the Hebrew Psalms as well as of what would now be called hymns.

[3] Parts of the "Te Deum" are probably of still earlier date. Cyprian (A.D. 252) makes an unmistakable quotation from it.

place to any great extent until the grand outburst of sacred song in the Western Church in the days of Ambrose and Augustine.

In like manner the materials for Christian devotion gathered and took form by degrees. The gifts of "the Spirit of grace and supplications" must have been long used and improved in the Churches ere those noble utterances took shape which we now find—mingled, indeed, with elements of error and superstition—in the liturgies of Jerusalem and Alexandria.[1] Such petitions and intercessions carried their own witness as given by the Spirit of prayer. They were felt to be fitting channels for the warmest and highest devotion. Some of them may have come from the prayers of the synagogue service, with Christian additions; others bear the stamp of the times of Roman persecution, such as the touching requests "for our fathers and brethren who are in captivity and exile, who are in mines, and under torture, and in bitter slavery." Such prayers won their way, first into the heart and memory of the Church, and then found their place in its earliest written forms of service.

Certain petitions, confessions and thanksgivings came into common use, and gathered round them hallowed associations in certain Churches, from

[1] These liturgies are conveniently accessible in the "Ante-Nicene Christian Library," vol. xxiv. (Clark's Series, Edin.).

their suitableness and beauty, and from their having been used by martyrs and confessors, or venerable and beloved ministers of Christ. One or two of the oldest liturgies now extant may thus, as regards some of their elements, go back to the fourth, or even to the third century. But they were then "oral, flexible, and varied." We must travel onwards from the days of our Lord over at least five hundred years, to a period of growing declension and decay, before we find anything like a system of prescribed and invariable prayers, making its appearance in the ordinary worship of the Christian Church.

The practical disadvantages of an enforced liturgy of this fixed and invariable stamp are very great. They are of a twofold kind, arising both from the inherent defects of the system itself, and from the general helplessness, and inability to go beyond the prayer-book on an emergency, which are seen in the ministers trained under the system. One or two concrete instances of this may perhaps bring out what I mean better than any general remarks.

Few names connected with the Episcopal Church of the United States are better known in this country than that of Dr. Phillips Brooks, rector of Trinity Church, Boston. At a recent congress of the American Episcopal Church, Dr. Brooks pled strongly for greater freedom in prayer, and gave this illustration of the evils of their present system :—A large Episcopal convention was assembled, when news came that a great city (Chicago ?) was on fire, and that thousands of people were houseless and exposed to extreme danger. With a natural and praiseworthy impulse, all agreed to adjourn the meeting, and to join in prayer for their fellow-countrymen suffering under such a calamity. The business in hand was adjourned accordingly, when, behold, a fatal difficulty emerged. There was no form of prayer in the Liturgy for such a case, and it was, of course, impossible to depart from it. The assembled bishops and clergy had to content themselves with going devoutly over the Litany, " laying before God almost every woe but the woe of a burning city." " Surely," the eloquent preacher went on, " bishops, clergy, and laity should have liberty to pour out their souls to God, wherever they be, for the very things they need, instead of compelling them to go in a roundabout way praying for other things, and trusting Omniscience to give them the things which are in their hearts ?" [1]

[1] *Catholic Presbyterian*, vii. 54. I noticed a similar case lately, reported in an American paper published in San Francisco. It had been arranged, it appears, in the English Episcopal Church of Yokohama, Japan, to have a day of special prayer for missions. Considerable pains had been taken to have a full meeting. The day arrived ; the people assembled early, but only to be told that it would be impossible to pray for

I give another illustration in the words of Professor Lorimer, of Edinburgh University, in his little treatise, "A National Church demands a National Liturgy"[1]:—

"There are few Episcopalians, I should think, who do not feel the entire exclusion of extempore prayer from the Liturgy of the Church of England to be a grave defect. We had a striking and very painful instance of its inconveniences quite recently. The Princess Alice died on a Saturday, in circumstances which called forth an outburst of universal grief and sympathy. On Sunday morning every heart was full, and every mouth would gladly have spoken. Yet in the metropolis of Scotland, where feelings of warm personal affection for the Royal Family, and for the Queen and Princess more especially, were exceptionally strong, even in the Church where the Bishop presided and preached, not the slightest reference was made to the sad event. As the Princess' name did not occur in the Liturgy, her death was not marked even by its omission, which was the only notice that was taken of her father's death (Prince Albert's) in similar circumstances. Surely even the pedantry of Ritualism need not exclude expressions of grief for the departed, or words of supplication for the bereaved. There was not a Presbyterian Church in Scotland, of any denomination, in which the Queen was not fervently prayed

missions that day, because the prayers had not arrived by the steamer! It was all the fault of the Bishop of London.

[1] Edinburgh, 1879, p. 33.

for on both occasions; and there was not a Presbyterian who, had not his lips been sealed by prejudice would not have said a fervent 'Amen.'"

Statements from Episcopalians to the same effect could be cited to almost any extent. "Could the prayer-book of the Irish Episcopal Church," asks an eloquent Irish writer, "express the agonised desires of the God-fearing people of that misguided land, when ferocious crimes were following one another too fast to be counted, through whole provinces, with anything approaching to the effect of sentences springing straight from the heart, and shaped by the very chisel of the events themselves?"[1]

All our readers will remember the painful interest awakened throughout Britain by the siege of Paris and the horrors of the Commune. No one can doubt that the members of the Church of England shared deeply in that interest, and would fain have expressed it in prayers such as the hearts of all Christians prompted, and in which men of all political views could have freely joined. But there was, of course, no provision for this in the Liturgy. Many suggested that a special prayer should be issued by authority. After some delay, there appeared in the papers an instructive correspondence between the Bishop of London and the Archbishop of Canterbury,

[1] *Catholic Presbyterian*, x. 267.

as to whether it would be possible to have some public prayer in reference to what was engaging so much thought and feeling in the country. It was decided that there was no precedent for it; and that it was impossible for the Church of England to pray about any war unless England herself was actually engaged in it. A form of prayer had been drawn up with the view of its being used in public. All that the two prelates could do in the circumstances, was to suggest that this prayer—a somewhat bald and meagre composition, as many thought—might be used by the people of the Church to help them in their private devotions.[1]

Fine as the funeral service of the Church of England is in many ways, you can hardly fail to see its defects, if you suppose yourself bound to use this formula at every grave, and to use nothing else. It contains, for example, no expression whatever of sympathy for the bereaved family or friends of the dead. It does not supply a single word of prayer for them in their affliction. A respected minister of our Church told me lately of an instance which occurred some years ago, in which he had been painfully struck with this. A young mother had died, leaving two infant children. She was much and justly beloved. Her husband was lying dan-

[1] See *Daily Review*, 9th Aug., 1870.

gerously ill at the time in a foreign land. The large company of near relatives and friends who gathered to the funeral, as well as the officiating clergyman himself, were under the full influence of the feelings naturally awakened by the touching circumstances. But there could not be one petition offered for blessing on the motherless children, nor for support and comfort to the bereaved husband and father under the sad tidings which were at that moment on their way to him. There had to be silence before God as to the very things which were most in the hearts of the mourners, because "it was not in the bond" by which prayer is straitened in the Church of England.

But do considerations such as these end the discussion which we have in hand regarding the duty of the Church as such in reference to the order and forms of public worship? Has the Reformed Church done her whole duty in this direction, when she protests, as she has good reason to do, against all enforced liturgies, and against all liturgies of the fixed and stereotyped kind with which we have now been dealing? Ought she to leave everything free in the matter of public worship? To that question we propose to address ourselves in the next chapter.

CHAPTER III.

THEORY AND PRACTICE OF SCOTTISH CHURCH AS TO PUBLIC WORSHIP: THE SCOTTISH METRICAL PSALMS: WESTMINSTER DIRECTORY FOR WORSHIP.

HAS the Reformed Church done her whole duty in reference to the order and forms of public worship, when she protests, as she has such good reason to do, against all enforced liturgies, and against all liturgies of the fixed and stereotyped kind with which we are familiar in the Church of England and in the Church of Rome? Ought she to leave everything free as regards the order and form of the stated services of God's House?

"No," would seem to be the answer given by the theory and practice of some Presbyterian Churches, the Scottish among the rest; "there are certain limits within which alone the freedom is to be exercised. The duty of the Church in this matter is threefold. First, let her state the New Testament elements of worship,—praise, prayer, the reading and exposition of the Scriptures, the preaching of the Gospel, the administration of the Sacraments. Secondly, let her provide her people with a psalm-book and a hymn-book, and some instruction in the use of them. Let them even have an organ, if they keep it in its right place, and do not quarrel over it. Thirdly, as to the presiding minister; let the Church give him full freedom within the limits now indicated, and exhort and encourage him to make the best use of it. Let him, with consent of the eldership of the congregation, combine and arrange the given elements of worship as he judges to be most for edification. In the matter of public prayer, in particular, let him meditate well beforehand, using what help of the pen he will to guide his thoughts. Let him consider the present circumstances and needs of his people, preparing his heart before God, stirring up himself to take hold of Him for them and with them, and then let him cast himself in faith on the promised help of the Spirit, and pray as God enables him to frame his words."

Such a system has many advantages. It proceeds upon the principle,—a true and noble one, —that if you appeal to Christian men by high motives to do great things, and expect them to do so, you will not generally be disappointed. Our Scottish Church, for example, by her plan of worship, calls upon each of her ministers to stir up the gift of God which is in him for all the work of the ministry to which he was solemnly set apart by prayer "with the laying on of the hands of the Presbytery."[1] She shows that she expects him not only to preach the Gospel, but to cultivate the power of leading the public worship of God in prayer in such a way as to edify the earnest and living members of the Church. He is thereby shut up, in a measure, by the very necessities of the case, to take heed to himself and to his own spiritual life, and to seek the spirit of true prayer. He thus learns to know, and to be thankful when he has in some degree attained to that spirit, to know, and to be humbled within himself, when he has come short of it.

The result has been that both now and in all periods in our history when there has been any amount of evangelical life in the Church, in other words, whenever there have been in existence the spiritual motives on which such an appeal counts, the response has never failed. There has been, with all our defects, a decidedly high average of attainment among the ministers of the Scottish Church, both in preaching and in the gift of edifying and acceptable public prayer.[2] And

[1] 1 Tim. iv. 14.
[2] I agree in this with what was said by Professor Bruce of Glasgow, at the Presbyterian Council in Philadelphia.—*Proceedings*, 131.

this, as regards prayer, has been reached in a way which, although difficult and sometimes depressing to the feelings of a young minister, has often been the means to him of no little blessing. He has found himself brought consciously "*en rapport*," in a very high sense, with the best of his people. There has been a true spiritual sympathy established between him and them, wonderfully elevating and supporting, as every minister can tell who has felt it,—not the less real and helpful because not expressed among us in the loud ejaculations and responses of our Methodist brethren.

As regards the Churches of the Westminster Confession we have, in theory at least, something more than this in the way of help and guidance for the minister; and, in practice, as regards the congregation, we have in the Scottish, Irish, and some of the American Churches, an ancient and admirable book of praise, which has done much to maintain the historic continuity and the sacred associations of Scottish worship. We have the Westminster Directory for the public worship of God; and we have the Scottish Metrical Psalms. Let us look first at the latter.

When, after the long spiritual darkness of the Middle Ages, light dawned again upon Europe in the sixteenth century, morning, as ever, brought gladness, and was hailed with song. Everywhere men broke loose from the trammels of a strange tongue, and of enforced silence in the Churches; and everywhere by a strong and true spiritual instinct recourse was had to the treasures of the Hebrew Psalter. The words of Chrysostom regarding the Church of his time were fulfilled again: "David in his Psalms is first, middle, and last in the assemblies of Christians." In Germany and Scotland, France and England, Holland, Switzerland, and Spain there appeared almost simultaneously during the early days of the Reformation, metrical versions of the Psalter, more or less complete, in the language of the common people.

From the standpoint of the Church of Rome in the fifteenth and sixteenth centuries, psalmody and heresy were convertible terms. The Lollards in England and Scotland took their very name from their psalm-singing. The French Psalms of Beza and Marot—first suggested by Calvin—spread like wildfire over France, and became one of the main badges and supports of the Huguenots during all the wars of the League. Strada, the Spanish Roman Catholic historian of the Low Countries, tells us that "the raising of a Geneva Psalm among the misbelievers was as if the trumpet had sounded a charge."

But, among all the metrical renderings of the Psalter which became current in the Reformed

Churches, the foremost place must undoubtedly be given to the Scottish version. It was published in its present form about two years after the close of the Westminster Assembly, after long and careful adjustment and revision by a well-chosen committee of ministers and elders appointed by the General Assembly of the Church of Scotland. The main body of the Psalms in common metre are taken in substance from the version which had been adopted by the Westminster Assembly as part of the proposed uniformity of worship in the three kingdoms, and which was written by Francis Rous, Provost of Eton, and Member of the Long Parliament. But it is by no means correct to ascribe to him, as is sometimes done, the sole authorship of the version published in 1650 by appointment of the General Assembly, and used thenceforth in Scotland. Not a few of the Psalms which it contains belong almost entirely to the version of Sir William Mure of Rowallan, and others to that of Alexander of Menstrie, afterwards Earl of Stirling, both of whom were well-known Scottish poets in the first half of the seventeenth century. But in many of its best features the Scottish Psalter goes back to the Reformation period. The Psalms which have the strongest hold on Scottish hearts, and which are linked with the most stirring scenes in our history, belong for the most part to the days of Knox. Thus, for example, the 100th Psalm, "All people that on earth do dwell," was written by William Keith, a Scottish exile in the reign of Queen Mary, and one of the translators of the Geneva Bible. The Old 124th, "Now Israel may say, and that truly," was composed by Whittingham, the brother-in-law of Calvin, who succeeded John Knox in the English pulpit at Geneva, and was afterwards Dean of Durham. The author of the "Second Versions" of Psalms 102, 136, 143 and 145 was John Craig, once a Dominican monk at Bologna, afterwards one of Knox's most trusted friends, who died minister of Holyrood and of the king's household.[1]

No version of the Psalms in any country has ever obtained a greater hold of the national mind and heart than the Scottish; none, probably, has so powerful an influence in the present day, and none better deserves it. Its faults lie on the surface. It is not unfrequently rough and

[1] See Dr. David Laing's valuable dissertation on this subject in Appendix to his edition of "Baillie's Letters and Journals," iii. 525-56; Livingston, *Scottish Metrical Psalter of* 1635, 27, 33. The same thing is true of many of the best and most popular of our Psalm tunes. They go back to the Reformation Church Psalters. Thus, for example, the three melodies named by Robert Burns in the "Cottar's Saturday Night" are "Martyrs," "Elgin," and "Dundee." They were the Psalm tunes commonly used by his father in family worship. And they belong, all three, to the days of Knox and Melville.

uncouth to modern ears. Some of its phrases and rhymes quoted in an isolated way may easily raise a smile. But, as a whole, it has surpassing merits, which are seen and felt the more carefully it is studied. In respect of faithfulness to the inspired original, in a certain high and grave simplicity, in strength and dignity, the Scottish Metrical Psalter is not unworthy of the name, given it by competent judges, of "the prince of versions." Rugged as its verses sometimes are, they are never weak. Along with its simple ballad metres, it has the noble directness, the unsought felicities of expression which mark the best of our Scottish ballads.[1] Passages meet you on almost every page which are fully equal in this respect to the *one* fine passage in the version of Sternhold and Hopkins, "The Lord descended from above, and bowed the heavens high." And it has been often remarked how, when the theme of the Psalm is the loftiest and most fitted for worship, the Scottish version seems to rise in power and beauty along with it.

This Psalter has gathered round it for Scottish

---

[1] It is on such grounds that Wordsworth, with the instinct of a true poet, brings in two lines from the Scottish version of the 88th Psalm as the dirge sung by the funeral procession among the mountains, which is described in a fine passage in the "Excursion":—

"Wilt Thou show wonders to the dead? Shall they rise and Thee bless?
Shall in the grave Thy love be known, in death Thy faithfulness?"

hearts the associations of all that is best and highest in our history for more than three hundred years. Every student of that history knows how these Psalms meet us in it again and again as the stay and solace of Christian men in hours of darkness and peril, as the natural utterance of joy and triumph. Our Scottish martyrs went to their doom with these Psalms upon their lips, echoed back by the sorrowing and awe-stricken crowds which gathered round the scaffold. It was with these Psalms to nerve them that Scottish peasants stood up fearlessly before the carabines of a savage soldiery at their own doors. And then, when the work was done, and the last file of troopers had disappeared over the muirland, women stole out in the darkening to dress the bodies, and that most touching of all melodies —" plaintive ' Martyrs,' worthy of the name,"— rose over them from trembling voices :—

"Their blood about Jerusalem like water they have shed;
And there was none to bury them when they were slain and dead.
*   *   *   *   *
Against us mind not former sins; Thy tender mercies show;
Let them prevent us speedily, for we're brought very low.
For Thy name's glory help us, Lord, who hast our Saviour been:
Deliver us; for Thy name's sake, oh, purge away our sin.

> Oh, let the prisoner's sighs ascend before Thy sight on high;
> Preserve those, in Thy mighty power, that are designed to die."

These were the Psalms that ascended from great Communion gatherings on the moors and hillsides in the days of the " Armed Conventicles."

> "Then rose the song, the loud
> Acclaim of praise; the wheeling plover ceased
> Her plaint; the solitary place was glad;
> And on the distant cairns the watcher's ear
> Caught doubtfully at times the breeze-borne note." [1]

This Scottish Psalter forms a wonderful bond of union and sympathy among Scotsmen all the world over. It is in fact a national liturgy of praise and prayer in the best sense of the word.[2]

---

[1] Graham, *The Sabbath*.

[2] Inseparably linked in this respect with the Psalter, are those fifteen or twenty noble hymns which, rising by their native virtue above the mass of the "Paraphrases," have for nearly a hundred and fifty years held a place in Scotland—except in the Highlands—second only to that of the Psalms. I refer to such hymns as "O God of Bethel," "Where high the heavenly temple stands," "'Twas on that night," "Hark, how the adoring hosts above," "How bright these glorious spirits shine." These were first printed by permission of the General Assembly in 1745, and had won their place in Scottish worship, along with the Psalms, for generations before a separate hymn-book was adopted by any Presbyterian Church in Scotland.—See Laing, *ubi supra*, p. 555. Acts of Assembly, 1745, vi. 9; 1747, 15th May; 1748, 21st May; 1750, 11; 1751, 10, &c.

Those who have had the privilege of ministering to their fellow-countrymen and country-women in the Colonies, or at sea, can testify to its power. They have seen and shared in the thrill that ran through the little gathering on shipboard, in the woods, or in the wilderness, and have seen tears come to eyes not prone to weeping, when the old Psalms were given out : " I to the hills," " O thou, my soul, bless God the Lord," " The Lord 's my Shepherd," " Pray that Jerusalem may have ; " and when there rose up from the little congregation the grave, sweet, familiar melody of " French," or " Coleshill," " Dunfermline," or " St. Paul's."

But let us turn now to the " Directory for the Public Worship of God, agreed upon by the Assembly of Divines at Westminster, with the assistance of Commissioners from the Church of Scotland, as a part of the Covenanted Uniformity in Religion betwixt the Churches of Christ in the kingdoms of Scotland, England, and Ireland." This is a document which deserves to be much more carefully studied than it usually is. It contains a great deal that is of very high and permanent value, both in the way of direct guidance, and of suggestion in matters of worship.[1]

---

[1] Nothing, for example, could be more admirable than the three general rules which it gives to a minister in the section "Of the Preaching of the Word," as to how he should handle

It cannot, however, be said to be of full authority even in the Churches which hold the Westminster Standards. Much of it has practically fallen into abeyance. Some of its rules are generally, or often, disregarded to our loss; as, for instance, its injunction that marriages should be celebrated in the Church, and its recommendation that the Lord's Prayer should be regularly used in public worship. One or two of its decisions, on the other hand, are now disregarded with advantage. Thus, for example, the Directory expressly enjoins that no service shall be held at funerals, either in the house or at the grave, referring as the reason for this to various abuses which had

his text. "His care ought to be : *First*, That the matter be the truth of God. *Secondly*, That it be a truth contained in *that* text. *Thirdly*, That he chiefly insist upon those doctrines which are principally intended, and make most for the edification of the hearers."

Hall, an Episcopalian writer, in a useful work, "Reliquiæ Liturgicæ" (5 vols., Bath, 1847), gives an account of the Westminster Assembly. It is a little coloured by denominational prepossessions, and exhibits some inaccuracies as to facts; but it is marked throughout by a sort of surprised candour. Of the "Directory for Public Worship," he says: "With all these deductions from its usefulness" (viz., "the rejection of the Apocrypha, the discontinuance of private baptism; of god-fathers and god-mothers; of the sign of the cross; of the wedding-ring," and other like things, which Mr. Hall feels to be serious defects), "the Directory is a fine composition, very simple, and often very solemn, and doubtless—by whomsoever composed—the result of no little thoughtfulness and care."—*Introd.* xxxviii.

arisen in connection with such observances. The former part of this prohibition has been almost from the first, in Scotland and elsewhere, universally disobeyed, and the latter part, especially of late years, very generally.[1]

In these circumstances, a careful revision and re-publication of the Directory by Church authority would be a very seasonable thing, and might in many ways lead to much good. It is obviously desirable that what is theoretically, to some extent, supposed to be the law of the Church as to public worship, and her actual practice in that department, should be brought into harmony with each other.

Practically, the main result of the Westminster Directory has been the general unwritten tradition of Scottish worship, which is based mainly upon it, although with distinct traces of the earlier system of the "Book of Common Order," where that was not followed at Westminster, and with evidence also of some later influences, to which I need not advert here. I refer to that "order of service," substantially the same over all Scotland to a wonderful extent, with which most of us in this country are so familiar. There are a few local variations, such as begin-

---

[1] See the excellent edition of the "Book of Common Order, and the Directory, with Historical Introductions and Notes," by Drs. Sprott and Leishman, Edin. 1868, 313, 318.

ning with a short prayer; which, by the way, ought to be the rule and not the exception, according both to the Book of Common Order and the Directory; but, speaking generally, the order is: Singing; prayer; reading of Scripture; singing (prayer); sermon (singing; Baptisms, if any); prayer; singing; benediction.

Beyond this unwritten "ordinance of the fathers,"—from which few young ministers would venture to vary, and still fewer would not speedily repent it if they did,—the pastor in a British or an American Presbyterian Church is practically left to himself as to what he reads from Scripture, as to the material, style, and length of his prayers, his order of Baptism and of the Communion, his marriage and funeral services.

Now, if our choice lay simply between this state of things, and our being bound hand and foot to a prayer-book after the fashion of the Church of England, I have no hesitation whatever in saying that we should remain as we are, and that for the reasons indicated in the second chapter of this little work. But the question at once suggests itself: Is there no middle ground? Does the Church do all her duty both to her ministers—especially her younger ministers—and to her people, which does no more in this department than is done at present by the Scottish and some other Presbyterian Churches?

Suppose you have an optional or discretionary liturgy, in connection with which free prayer shall not only be permitted, but positively *enjoined* and set in the place of honour; such a service-book, with improvements, as Knox and Calvin framed at Geneva, and the Church of Scotland used for a hundred years after; such a liturgy as the Waldensian Church possesses,[1] and as the Dutch Reformed Church uses to this day, both in its Dutch and in its English-speaking branches in Europe, Africa, and America,—what are the advantages and disadvantages of such a plan as compared with that which prevails in those British and American Churches with which we are more familiar?

[1] "La Liturgie Vaudoise, ou la Manière de Célébrer le Service Divin, comme elle est établie dans l'Église Evangélique des Vallées du Piémont. Par ordre du Synode." The copy of this liturgy which lies before me was presented, as the inscription upon it bears, "to the Library of the Free Church of Scotland at Edinburgh, by the Moderator of the Waldensian Church, M. Bonjour, pastor of the parish of St. Germain, 15th July, 1844." The Synod, or Supreme Court of the Waldensian Church, appointed a committee in 1878 to revise this liturgy, and bring it more into accordance with the present needs of all their congregations both in the Valleys and in Italy. The revised Service-book is to be submitted for approval to the Synod which meets in September, 1884.

CHAPTER IV.

LITURGIES OR BOOKS OF COMMON ORDER AS USED BY THE MAJORITY OF THE REFORMED CHURCHES: DANGERS AND ADVANTAGES.

THE point raised at the close of last chapter was this: Suppose you have an optional or discretionary liturgy, in connection with which free prayer is not only permitted, but expressly enjoined and set in the place of honour,—what are the advantages and disadvantages of such a plan, as compared with that which now prevails in most of the British and American Presbyterian Churches?

There can be no question at all events,—except among the ignorant,—as to its being a lawful arrangement for the "seemly form and order"[1] of the public worship of God in a Presbyterian Church.[2] In fact, the weight of precedent is all

---

[1] The εὐσχημοσύνη καὶ εὐταξία referred to in 1 Cor. xiv. 40.

[2] Compare Dr. Charles Hodge's strong statements to this effect, in his chapter on "Presbyterian Liturgies" in *The Church and its Polity*, Lond. 1879, 156. So also Ebrard, in the Appendix to his valuable "Collection of Prayers and Liturgical Formularies used in the Reformed Church," expresses his surprise at finding

on that side. We in Scotland, since the middle of the seventeenth century, have placed ourselves in quite an exceptional position among the Churches of the Reformation in not having such an optional liturgy. It was only at the Westminster Assembly that the Church of Scotland gave up the one she had hitherto employed, embodying the prayers and forms of service for Baptism and the Lord's Supper, for marriage, &c., which had been used by John Knox and Andrew Melville, by Alexander Henderson and Samuel Rutherford. She did this not from any doubt as to the lawfulness and value of her own liturgy or Book of Common Order; but, to a large extent, in a spirit of catholicity for which she has not received enough of credit, to meet the preferences of the English Puritan divines who formed the majority of the Westminster Assembly. They had suffered for years under the heavy yoke of the English prayer-book and canons, sternly enforced with Star-Chamber penalties by men like Bancroft, Wren, and Laud. It was no wonder that

in the course of his researches that "the Scottish Church has no liturgical formularies at all, not even a formulary for Baptism and the Lord's Supper, but leaves everything free to the clergyman. The Church festivals also have been wholly given up by her; she has only the Sunday. The Reformed Church of Hungary, too, has no definite liturgy."—*Reformirtes Kirchenbuch; vollständige, Sammlung der in der reformirten Kirche eingeführten Kirchengebete und Formulare*, Zürich, 1847, 290.

there was something of a reaction in their minds against liturgies of any kind whatever. And the Scottish Commissioners, having before them the grand ideal of a united Reformed Church for all the three kingdoms, yielded in this, as on some other points, to the prevailing feeling of their English brethren.[1] But no one in the Westminster Assembly, except the little group of Independents,—" the five Dissenting Brethren," as they were called,—ever dreamed of denying the *lawfulness*, and, in some circumstances, the *expediency* of an optional liturgy.

Listen to a Presbyterian divine, who was in high esteem among those who sat in the Jerusalem Chamber at Westminster,—Edwards, the author of the " Antapologia " and the " Gan-

---

[1] See, *e.g.*, "The General Assembly's answer to the Right Reverend the Assembly of Divines in the Kirk of England," in reference to their acceptance of the Westminster Directory in 1645. " In other particulars," they say, after some reservations about the mode of receiving the Lord's Supper; "we have resolved and do agree to do as ye have desired us in your letter; that is, not to be tenacious of old customs though lawful in themselves, and not condemned in this Directory, but to lay them aside for the nearer uniformity with the Kirk of England, now nearer and dearer to us than ever before; a blessing so much esteemed and so earnestly longed for among us, that, rather than it fail on our part, we do most willingly part with such customs and practices of our own as may be parted with safely, and without the violation of any of Christ's ordinances or trespassing against Scriptural rules or our solemn Covenants."—*Acts of Assembly* (*Church Law Soc. ed.*) 131.

græna." He is replying to an Independent writer: "Whereas you say, 'There is this great controversy upon the ordinance of public worship about the lawfulness of set forms prescribed,' I must tell you 'this great controversy' upon it is raised only by yourselves (the five dissenting brethren), and the Brownists; there being no divines, and no Reformed Churches that I know of, but do allow the lawful use of set forms of prayer, composed and framed by others—as by Synods and Assemblies—and do make use of such sometimes, as the Churches of France and Holland in the administration of Sacraments usually do; and those who practise them not so much, yet at least hold them lawful. And I challenge you in all your reading to name one divine of note and orthodox that ever held set forms of prayer unlawful, excepting only Independents."[1]

Beside this, we may place the view of a more modern theologian, the late Dr. John Duncan of the New College, Edinburgh: "I do not wonder that the desire for forms of prayer is returning. I could say nothing against the use of a liturgy as a catholic question for all the Churches. But I am definite against confinement to it; and as for us in Scotland, I am opposed to it in any form at present." (This was said about twenty-five years ago.) "But a good liturgy forms a

[1] Edwards, *Antapologia*, Lond. 1644, 98f.

fine common bond for the Churches. I remember when in Leghorn hearing a very painful sermon from the Bishop of ———; and on leaving the church, a friend remarked, 'I'm thankful he can't spoil the prayers.' . . . The cultus of the Ritualist and of the old Scotch Seceder are at opposite extremes. In the one we have the external form, often without the internal spirit. In the other we have the internal element, without the smallest regard to its outward form. But it is the ghost and the body together that make the man."[1]

Assuming, then, what really cannot be denied with any show of reason, that on grounds of Scripture, and from the standpoint of the

[1] *Colloquia Peripatetica*, Edin. ed. 1870, 32, 114. It is interesting to observe that the mind of Dr. Chalmers seems to have been turning in the same direction. It is well known that he often wrote and read his own prayers on public occasions. In a preface written by him to a collection of prayers, largely taken from John Knox's liturgy, Baxter, Leighton, Scougal, and other old writers, Dr. Chalmers says: "The attempt has been long made to improve the psalmody of our Church by means of a new collection for it. There are two distinct methods of accomplishing this object, either by means of original sacred poetry, or by a compilation from the existent sacred poetry. Without superseding the former, we confess our preference for the latter method; and it is a preference we are disposed to extend from a Book of Psalms or Hymns to a Book of Prayers, which, while interspersed with new compositions, might be mainly formed from the pious effusions of many different minds that were the lights of the Church in different ages."—Cochrane, *Manual of Family and Private Devotion, with Preface by Dr. Chalmers*, 3rd ed. p. 4.

Reformed Church Catholic, an optional or discretionary liturgy is a perfectly lawful thing for any Church to adopt, let us consider what is to be said of it on grounds of expediency. What are its advantages and disadvantages?

I. One objection is sure to be raised in some quarters: "It is un-Presbyterian. Our forefathers were all against liturgies. Jenny Geddes threw a stool at a Dean because he began to read a liturgy in St. Giles."

In answer to that, I have simply to say that the objection rests upon an utter ignorance of history in this matter, and upon an inability to distinguish things that differ. The Presbyterian Churches of the Reformation—in other words, *all* the Churches of the Reformation, except the Church of England—were unanimous in favour of an optional liturgy. At this moment the Presbyterian Churches which have a liturgy are far more in number than those which have not.

What the Covenanters of 1637-38 were against was a Popish liturgy, forced upon them in an Erastian way. That was why Jenny Geddes was so emphatic about "the mass" being said "at her lug." But the Covenanters of 1637 were not against *all* liturgies, for the very good reason that they had a liturgy of their own, which they had no intention at that time of giving up. The morning prayers of that liturgy had been read in St. Giles as usual, on the morning of the eventful 23rd of July, by Mr. Patrick Henderson. He was a respected member of the party afterwards known as that of the Covenanters, and was so much opposed to the new liturgy that he had deliberately incurred the loss of the position and emoluments of Reader in St. Giles, which he had enjoyed for many years, rather than countenance the innovations.[1] Many good women — Jenny Geddes herself in all likelihood among them—had been joining devoutly in the prayers which had been read that morning, as had been the case in that Church ever since John Knox was minister in it.[2]

[1] "Mr. Patrick Henderson, Reader in the Great Kirk of Edinburgh, refused to read it (an edict regarding the introduction of Laud's Service-book); and for this both the Bishop and Council of Edinburgh assured him he behoved to quit his place, whilk he condescended unto. Yet he continued all that week in saying of the prayers (of Knox's Service-book), and the next Sabbath, still shedding many tears, considering the deplorable condition of God's Kirk; so that many of the people were much commoved with his demeanour, considering also that he who had been so long in that place and had acquitted himself so faithfully and diligently in it, and who was known to be a lover of the truth, now behoved to be put from his place for the discountenancing of corruption entering into the Kirk of God.

"When the next Sabbath, 23rd July, came, the Bishop of Edinburgh, *after that the ordinar prayers had been read in the morning*, about ten o'clock brought in the Service-book to the pulpit."—Row, *History of the Kirk of Scotland*, Wodrow ed. 408.

[2] It is interesting to remember that he used these prayers in his family also when shut out by infirmity from public worship.

That was no reason at all, of course, why they and their fellow-countrymen and women should consent for a moment to have Laud's Service-book and Canons thrust upon the Church and people of Scotland against their will. But so far as history and Presbyterianism are concerned, if we went back to an optional liturgy like John Knox's Book of Common Order, we would only be going back to the oldest Presbyterian ways, to the practice of the first and second Reformation in Scotland. And it was English influence, not Scottish, at the Westminster Assembly that led to the change.

In point of fact, it was one of the "grievances" of the Covenanters in 1637 that the bishops had issued a prohibition of the old Service-book. If the Scottish people would not accept the new one from England, they should have none at all. Hear John Row of Carnock, a contemporary witness, and a Presbyterian of the Presbyterians. "All this week," he complains, "there was no public worship in Edinburgh, neither sermon nor prayers read morning and evening, as the custom was. Yea, for five or six months after this, Mr. Patrick Henderson read not the prayers." . . .

The last prayer in which John Knox joined on earth was the "Evening Prayer," given at the end of the Book of Common Order. It was read at family worship in his chamber about an hour before he died. See Appendix A.

"*29th July.*—The Bishops ordain that neither old nor new Service be in public, except sermon, till the King's Majesty's mind be known on this late tumult." [1]

The petitions which came to the Privy Council in Edinburgh from ministers in Ayrshire and elsewhere, " upon a motion first made by Mr. David Dickson, minister at Irvine, to his Presbytery," request that the Church and her ministers should not have the new Service-book and Canons intruded upon them, " declaring, at the same time, that they were ready to alter everything

---

[1] Row, *History*, 410, 483. The report of the Archbishop of St. Andrews to the Privy Council, "anent the Service-book," "for himself and in name of the remanent Bishops," may be seen in the Appendix to Baillie's Letters. It is to the effect stated above, i. 448; *Records of the Kirk of Scotland*, (Peterkin), 52. In the Register House, Edinburgh, there are preserved forty-six of the petitions sent in from burghs, parishes, and presbyteries against Laud's Service-book. Several extracts from these are given by Drs. Sprott and Leishman, in the Introduction to their edition of the Book of Common Order and Directory:—"We having, for the form of worship according to God's own Word, established among us, Acts of Parliaments and General Assemblies yet standing, and have found the sensible blessing of God in the exercise thereof so long enjoyed, to our great comfort and edification." "Far different from that Book of Common Prayer which we have enjoyed many years," &c. "In none of them," the editors state, "have we observed any reference to the question of a liturgy as such, whether discretionary or prescribed, though they all complain of the imposition of Laud's book as the only form of public worship in the kingdom."—P. 28.

that could be made appear by any man to be unsound in the form of discipline and liturgy which they had received from their ancestors. They pointed out the principal heads of error contained in these books (*i.e.*, Laud's), and offered to dispute, or rather converse, in a friendly way about them. . . . They observed also those unhappy controversies whereby the Church was oppressed in the reign of Charles the Great, while some adhered to the Ambrosian liturgy, others, in place thereof, promoting the Gregorian or Roman; and with what calamities the kingdom of Spain was in former times shaken under the reign of Alphonso VI., who, by the advice of the Pope's legate, proposed to suppress the ancient Mozarabic liturgy, that he might in place thereof introduce the Gregorian, while all ranks of the kingdom were reclaiming against it."[1]

The prohibition by the prelates of the use of the old Scottish liturgy, or Book of Common Order, formed part of the indictment against them at their trial before the Glasgow Assembly in 1638. At the close of that trial, Alexander Henderson, as Moderator, was called upon to pronounce the solemn sentence of deposition and excommunication in presence of the Assembly,

[1] Stevenson, *History of the Church and State of Scotland from* 1625 *to* 1649: Edin. 1840, 172.

and of an immense audience, in the old Cathedral of Glasgow. Before doing so, he instructed the clerk, Johnstone of Warriston, to read aloud, for the information of all men, an abstract of what, after long and careful trial, had been found proven against the bishops. After this had been done, the Moderator singled out some of the main points, and impressed these upon the general audience. Apart from charges of immorality, the prelates had been tried and found guilty for three main offences : "For the superstition and idolatry they brought into the worship of God; for the tyranny they brought into the government of the Church ; and for the heresy they brought in upon doctrine." Under the head of offences connected with the public worship of the Church, Henderson lays special stress on "their interdicting Morning and Evening Prayers," as well as on "their bringing in innovations in the worship of God, such as the superstitious Service-book, tyrannous Book of Canons, and Book of Ordination." "For these and many other gross transgressions and slanders, at length expressed and clearly proven in their process, which are not seemly to be named in this place; and instead of their repentance, adding to all these evils extreme contempt of this Church, declining and protesting against this honourable, reverend, and duly constitute Assembly, they have incurred and justly deserve this fearful sentence of excommunication." [1]

II. But it may be said: "Granting that the historical facts are as you have stated them, still for more than two centuries the British and most of the American Presbyterian Churches have had no liturgy. They have flourished without one, at least as well as other branches of the Reformed Church, on the Continent of Europe and elsewhere, whose worship has always been more or less liturgical. Why should we in this country change our ground now in this matter, and borrow forms and prayers that belong to the Church of England? Is it not a movement in the wrong direction? Does it not savour of a tendency towards the external and ceremonial rather than the spiritual? Besides, practically, if you bring in anything of this kind, will you not play into the hands of the Episcopalians? If people want a liturgy, they will go to the Church of England or to the Church of Rome."

In reply to such objections, I admit at once that a liturgy of any kind may be a snare to an individual or to a Church. It may cover spiritual sloth and deadness. The desire for it may spring, in some instances, from a tendency to externalism in religion. But these dangers and disadvantages exist to a far greater extent

---

[1] *Records of the Kirk of Scotland*, 179f.

in the case of a fixed and enforced liturgy than in the case of an optional one, especially if in connection with it free prayer is not only theoretically allowed, but positively enjoined and set in the place of honour. Now this latter plan is the old historic position of the Reformed Church in Scotland and all the world over. I believe that it is, on the whole, the safest and strongest position, as between risks and extremes on either side.

No wiser and more competent exponent of the position in question could be found than Alexander Henderson, the great leader of the Church of Scotland in the days of the Covenant. He was fully aware of the dangers which lie in opposite directions in this matter. It was he who led the opposition to Laud's Service-book in the Synod of Fife and in the east of Scotland generally, as Dickson of Irvine did in the west. It was Henderson's petition to the Privy Council on the subject, in August, 1637, which first drew the eyes of all men to him at Court as well as throughout the country, and which marked out with masterly skill and clearness the position taken and held by the Church in all the subsequent struggles. In his petition, a document of characteristic weight and brevity, he rests his cause on the broad grounds of the spirituality and freedom of the Church, and the Popish character of the new liturgy, which it was proposed to thrust upon her without authority either from the General Assembly or from Parliament, and against the will of her ministers and people. But in an accompanying paper, intended for the consideration of individual members of Council, Henderson goes somewhat more into detail. He brings forward seven brief objections to the Service-book; the sixth of these refers to its compulsory character, and its not only discouraging but excluding free prayer in public worship: "It establisheth a reading ministry,—whosoever can read the Book can be a minister; and he who is best-gifted must say no more than he readeth, whether in prayer, Baptism, Communion, &c."[1]

But, on the other hand, none were more decided than Alexander Henderson in opposition to that tendency towards the views and practices in worship of the English Independents or Brownists, which began to show itself in the Scottish Church some two years after the Glasgow Assembly, and to which such frequent and disapproving references are made by Principal Baillie in his letters. In connection with that tendency some "discountenanced read prayers," and "scunnered at the Lord's Prayer and the Belief." They also encouraged private conventicles, at which various irregularities took

[1] Baillie, i. 449-51.

place, and objected to the custom of the minister kneeling for private devotion in the pulpit before beginning the public service, to the use of the doxology at the close of the Psalms, and to some other usages of the Reformed Church in Scotland.[1] " Divers of our chief ministers," Baillie writes in 1640, " tendering very much the credit of these very pious people, were loath that anything concerning them should come in public. We had sundry private meetings with the chief that were thought to incline that way. Mr. Henderson vented himself, at many occasions, passionately, opposed to all these conceits."

Henderson, indeed, by his consistent opposition to these " novations," drew upon himself considerable displeasure from many who were attracted by the spiritual warmth and earnestness of some who practised them. " Some citizens of Edinburgh declared themselves not well satisfied with Mr. Henderson's zeal against their practice. One Livingstone, a trafficker with the English who were affected to our

[1] Baillie, i. 249-55, 362f.; *Records of the Kirk*, 286f. 304. The "Gloria Patri" or doxology at the end of each of the Metrical Psalms was a feature in various editions of the old Scottish Psalter which was bound up with the Book of Common Order. These "Conclusions," as they were called, were given in every variety of metre in which the Psalms themselves were rendered—thirty-two in all.—See Livingston, *Scottish Metrical Psalter of* 1635. Glasgow, 1864, 35f.

Reformation, but withal to the discipline of New England, in his letter to his friends abroad, did write very despitefully of Mr. Henderson; this being intercepted did grieve not only the man himself, but us all, of all ranks, who had found him the powerful instrument of God, fitted expressly, much above all others, to be a blessing to our Church in this most dangerous season."[1]

The matter came up, in one form or other, at several Assemblies. In one of them a resolution was proposed, "That read prayer was not unlawful." This was amended by David Dickson of Irvine, to the stronger statement, "That it should be lawful to read prayers both in private and public."[2] At the Assembly of 1641, a conference on the subject was held in the Earl of Loudon's chambers in Edinburgh, by invitation of two other leading elders of the Church, the Marquis of Argyll and the Earl of Cassilis. Alexander Henderson, George Gillespie, Samuel Rutherford, David Dickson, Robert Blair, David Calderwood, Andrew Cant, and other distinguished men were present. Baillie, who was there, gives a full account. Some of the brethren, "who were suspected of innovating, did purge themselves fully of all such intentions." The innovations complained of were enumerated by Mr. Andrew Ramsay, one of the

[1] Baillie i. 250.   [2] i. 253.

ministers of Edinburgh: " Omitting 'Glory to the Father' and kneeling in the pulpit, discountenancing read prayers, and the rest. They gave answer to satisfaction, that betwixt us and them there was no discrepancy at all. At last, Mr. Henderson fell on that model, which thereafter was voiced and printed. This happy concord, whereof Argyll and Mr. Henderson were the happy instruments, will, we trust, have a great blessing to this whole land, which everywhere began to be fashed with idle toys and scruples."[1]

[1] i. 362. As minister of Kilwinning, Baillie had had his own share of the "fasherie" to which he refers. "Three or four yeomen of my flock refused to sing the Conclusion"—*i.e.*, the doxology. Baillie has left in writing "the sum of his conference" or private interview and reasoning with them about their difficulty. He ascribes it without hesitation, it will be observed, to alien influences. "If you have so readily embraced the scruples which private men and strangers have cast in your mind about this one point, beware that this dispose not your hearts to embrace more of their evil seed. I forewarn you, the rejecting of the Conclusion is one of the first links of the whole chain of Brownism. We have oft seen from this beginning seducers in this land have drawn on their followers to scunner at and reject our whole Psalms in metre; and then to refuse our Prayers, then our Sacraments, then our preaching, then at last our Church, our Covenant, and all. . . . Wherefor, as you would be loath to cast away your whole Psalms; as you would be loath to give up your Prayers, Sacraments, preaching; as you would not forsake wholly our Church and your sworn Covenant, and drink down all the errors of Brownism, take heed to your spirit, whilk you find so ready to learn the first lessons of these seducers. . . . 'It is (you say) a human Popish invention.' We deny it to be so; for we have given good Scriptural grounds

A very interesting little treatise, on the "Government and Order of the Church of Scotland," was written by Alexander Henderson in 1641. It was a sort of manifesto on the part of the Scottish Commissioners to the Westminster Assembly, designed to correct mistakes which they found to be not uncommon in England regarding the polity and worship of the Scottish Church. One of the statements current was that the Scots "had no certain rule or direction for their public worship, but that every man, following his extemporary fancy, did preach or pray what seemed good in his own eyes." A similar charge had been made before by Dr. Balcanquhal, in a document known as the "Large Declaration," and had been stigmatised by the Assembly in 1639, along with a number of other statements in the same production, as false and calumnious.[1] It is refuted also by Henderson in the treatise to which I now refer. "Against this accusation," he says, "the form of Prayers, administration of the Sacraments, admission of ministers, excommunica-

for it. We grant it is part of the (English) Liturgy and Mass-book too. But this proves it not be any worse than the Lord's Prayer and the Belief, which are both in these evil books. True, the Brownists will teach you to scunner at both; yet they will grant that many things in the Liturgy and Mass-book also are no more the worse for standing in those evil places than the sunbeams for shining on a dunghill."—Livingston, *ubi supra*, 36.

[1] *Records of the Kirk of Scotland*, 265f.

tion, solemnising of marriage, visitation of the sick, &c., which are set down before their Psalm-book, and to which the ministers are to conform themselves, is a sufficient witness: for although they be not tied to set forms and words, yet are they not left at random; but for testifying their consent and keeping unity, they have their Directory and prescribed Order." Again, in replying to a charge of enmity to monarchical government, Henderson appeals to the authorised liturgy of the Church of Scotland, as well as to her other standards: "Their Confession of Faith, the Doctrine and Prayers of their Church, their late Declarations and Remonstrances, express as much respect and reverence to magistracy as any Christian Prince will require." [1]

Additional evidence could be easily given to show that the historical position of the Scottish Church in this matter, deliberately taken up by her best representatives both at the first and second Reformation, was that of a discretionary liturgy, regarded and used as at once a basis, guide, and stimulus for the exercise of free prayer on the part of her ministers, elders, and people. Certainly we should not borrow the dress or the ornaments of other Churches of an alien stock. There are few things more objec-

---

[1] *Government and Order of Church of Scotland*, 1641. *To the Reader*, 3f.

tionable than to find scraps from the English Prayer-book forming a sort of mosaic with the feeble prose of a young minister's prayer. But why should we not wear, in our own fashion, the common garb of that great family of the Churches of the Reformation to which we belong? Why should we not develop the native Church order of our own Church in the matter of worship, wisely and cautiously, on its own historic lines?[1]

Few people are aware, for instance, that in the last decade of the sixteenth century, when the Church of Scotland was in the very flower of its Presbyterianism, and the star of Andrew Melville rode highest, there were in use here by Church authority no fewer than one hundred and forty-nine collects. They are printed in the edition of the Book of Common Order, published in 1595,[2] the same in which the full set

[1] Comp. Ebrard, *Reformirtes Kirchenbuch*, iv.

[2] The general title of the book is, "The CL. Psalms of David in Metre, with Prayers and Catechism according to the Form used in the Kirk of Scotland: Edinburgh, Henry Charteris, 1595." It has a double date, the prose part of the volume being dated 1596. The two parts might be sold separately; the object being, as stated in the Preface, "the ease of men in travel, and being from their home, who gladly would carry a thin book, as this of the Prayers is, that cannot easily carry the whole Psalms." The General Assembly kept a vigilant eye upon all alterations of the prayers in their authorised formularies. Twice over, in 1638 and 1640, Raban, an Aberdeen printer, was called to account by the Assembly for some verbal changes made by him in one of the prayers in his edition of

of the doxologies first appeared, under the name of "Prayers on the Psalms." But they are regular collects, and many of them of a very high order, marked by great power and chasteness of expression, and framed upon the most approved model for a collect, each having an "Invocation," a "Petition," and a "Conclusion." They are, I have little doubt, among the prayers specially referred to by Alexander Henderson, half-a-century after their publication. He had been asked by the General Assembly to draft a new form of service in which the Churches of England and Scotland might agree, but, with his usual wisdom, declined the task, for two main reasons: First, because such a movement, to be successful, must be initiated by the two Churches together, and the Scottish Church, in particular, ought carefully to avoid even the appearance of dictating to the English; but, secondly, "I

the Book of Common Order.—Sprott and Leishman, xviii.f. Comp. Acts of Assembly, 1601, 16th May, in *Book of the Universal Kirk of Scotland*, 497. It was of the year after that in which these collects appeared that Calderwood writes: "This year (1596) is a remarkable year to the Church of Scotland, both for the beginning and for the end of it. The Church of Scotland was now come to her perfection, and the greatest purity that ever she attained unto, both in doctrine and discipline, so that her beauty was admirable to foreign Churches. The assemblies of the saints were never more glorious nor profitable to every one of the true members thereof than in the beginning of this year.—*Hist.* (Wodrow ed.), v. 387.

F

could not," he said, "take upon me to set down other forms of prayer than we have in our Psalm-book, penned by our great and divine Reformers."[1]

It is true that the strength of our Presbyterian Church as regards its worship, apart from preaching, has lain in its spirituality, its Scriptural freedom and power of adaptation to circumstances, and in a certain grave and dignified simplicity. This has always been recognised by all who were competent to discern and appreciate such features in worship. "I hope," Mr. Gladstone said, writing in January, 1883, to a minister of the United Presbyterian Church, "that the tendency in Scotland to an increase of ritual will not be indulged without reserve; for there was a solemn and stern simplicity in the old form of Presbyterian worship, which was entitled to great respect, and which was a thing totally different from the mean nakedness and the cold worldliness and indifference so widely dominant in English services fifty years ago."[2]

This is a needful warning. But what is implied in the suggestion of an optional liturgy of the type of the Book of Common Order would not, if rightly and deliberately gone about, impair the simplicity and elasticity of our

---

[1] Baillie, ii. 2. For some specimens of these Scottish Collects of 1595, see Appendix B.

[2] Letter to the Rev. Andrew Duncan, Author of *The Scottish Sanctuary, as it was and as it is:* Hawarden, 3rd January, 1883.

service, and would very specially guard its dignity. Think, for example, how marriage services and Baptisms are often conducted by Presbyterian ministers, who do not even guide themselves by the Directory for Worship. Can anything more undignified be easily conceived? Think how not unfrequently the solemnity of the Lord's Table is marred, and the edification of the communicants hindered, by rambling, diffuseness, and irrelevancy in prayer and address. In most of the cases to which I refer, these evils would have been averted, or very greatly lessened, had the Church set some high and simple model of such services before the young minister, which he might use, or upon which he might mould himself, before his ministerial habits were formed, and before a fatal facility of slovenly utterance was acquired.

III. But an objector may say: "Argue as plausibly as you will from a theoretical point of view; practically, the two systems of liturgy and free prayer cannot live together. You must make your choice between the one and the other, with the benefits and the drawbacks attaching to each respectively. It is like the relation between the system of endowments for a Church, and the system of support by voluntary Christian liberality. Theoretically, one would suppose that an endowed Church, being saved the burden of upholding her own ministry and Church fabrics, would do so much the more for other objects. But, practically, the reverse seems to be true. The unendowed Churches both support themselves, and do much more for missions at home and abroad than their wealthier neighbours who are established by the State. So, practically, a Prayer-book established in the Church would kill free prayer. It has done so in the Church of England and in the Scotch Episcopal Communion. Young ministers would turn what was meant to be a staff into a crutch, and would never learn to walk alone. They would lean wholly upon a liturgy, if you gave them one, even of a nominally optional kind, and would fail to cultivate the gift and grace of free prayer."

Now, I have always felt this to be a weighty argument. It is perfectly conclusive, even if it stood alone, against a liturgy of the Anglican type; and it ought to be very carefully weighed as bearing against even an optional liturgy. Considerations of this kind are urged by Hog of Carnock in a temperate but powerful way, and in a very warm and evangelical spirit, in a little treatise written in 1710.[1] They do not seem

[1] *Letter on the Unlawfulness of Imposing Forms of Prayer*, Edin. 1710, 10-13, 25ff., 42-67. Prof. Henry Drummond gives an impressive warning against dangers of a spiritual kind arising for members as well as ministers of the Church, both in cases where all other parts of worship are subordinated to the sermon

to me to be conclusive against the old position of the Reformed Church in this matter; but they certainly indicate dangers and abuses which may arise in connection with it, and which should be carefully guarded against by suitable means.

On the other hand, it is to be remembered: *First*, that many a slothful, unspiritual minister gets by degrees into a stereotyped form of prayer under the present system. By a combination of tradition and haphazard, his individual "offices" take shape,—"if shape it may be called, that shape hath none,"—and are soon only too well known to his unfortunate flock. You have there, on a small scale, all the evils of a fixed liturgy, with none of its advantages.[1]

Secondly, the evidence of experience proves that an optional liturgy, if framed on sound principles, and used by the Church in a right

and in cases where the service is largely or wholly liturgical. —*Natural Law in the Spiritual World*, 2nd ed. 352f.

[1] I have been credibly informed of one "Moderate" minister in the far North, who had literally only *one* prayer in public worship. It was repeated Sabbath after Sabbath without the slightest variation. Once a-year, on the occasion of the yearly Communion, there was one additional sentence; that was the sole change of which it was capable. Naturally, the spiritual life of the parish passed over to "The Secession." Some little urchins at the parish school, who were sometimes stigmatised in the playground as "Blue Seceders," used to avenge themselves upon their comrades of "the Auld Kirk" by repeating, with perfect accuracy and amazing volubility, "Daddy ——'s prayer."

way, can exist side by side with, and indeed contribute to a very remarkable development of the gift of free prayer. John Knox's liturgy, for example, did not hinder, but helped and guided such a development in the Scottish Church during the first century after the Reformation. The prayers of the Book of Common Order were regularly read in the Church of St. Giles, Sabbath and week-day, under Knox's own ministry and that of his successors there. By the General Assembly which met in December, 1564, "It was ordained that every minister, exhorter, and reader shall have one of the Psalm-books lately printed in Edinburgh, and *use the order contained therein in Prayers, Marriage, and ministration of the Sacraments.*"[1] But the Book of Common Order, which they were thus instructed to use, not only allowed but *enjoined* the minister to go beyond the forms which it supplied. The prayer before the sermon was to be always free, no form for it being given. As regards the

---

[1] *Book of the Universal Kirk*, i. 54; "Knox's Works" (Laing's ed.) vi. 279. Comp. *First Book of Discipline*, chap. xi. 1, 2, as to the importance attached to "the Common Prayers," and the expediency of there being "in great towns *every day*, either sermon or common prayers, with some exercise of reading of Scriptures." It is worth noting, however, that in the same paragraph the place and honour due to free prayer are specially guarded.

special offices for the Communion, Baptism, and Marriage, the rubrics were stricter. Certain parts of these services were fixed, while liberty was left as to varying others. But as regards the ordinary worship of the Lord's Day, the discretionary and stimulating character of the Liturgy was emphasised throughout. The following are some of its rubrics: "The minister useth one of these two Confessions, or like in effect, exhorting the people diligently to examine themselves, following in their hearts the tenor of his words." "The people sing a Psalm all together, to a plain tune; which ended, the minister prayeth for the assistance of God's Holy Spirit, as the same shall move his heart, and so proceedeth to the sermon," ... "which ended, he either useth the 'Prayer for all Estates' before mentioned, or else prayeth as the Spirit of God shall move his heart, framing the same according to the time and matter which he hath entreated of."[1] The old Scottish Liturgy, in short, was framed upon wise and Scriptural principles; and the natural fruits followed. It was not a hindrance, but a help and guide to the exercise and cultivation of the gift of free prayer throughout the Church.

Take the case of one of the most eminent and

---

[1] Dunlop, *Collection of Confessions*, ii. 417, 421, 426; *Book of Common Order* (Sprott and Leishman) xxii. 79, 86, 90.

gifted of Knox's successors in St. Giles, Robert Bruce of Kinnaird. The prayers of the old Liturgy were read statedly under his ministry in the ordinary services of the Church. When banished to Inverness early in the seventeenth century, for faithfulness to conscience and for opposing the innovations of the Court and the prelatic party, "he remained there four years," Calderwood writes, "teaching every Sabbath before noon, and every Wednesday, and read the prayers every other night at even." "He exhorted at the prayers," another account says, "every evening while there." The result of his work and influence at Inverness was a general revival of spiritual religion in the whole town and neighbourhood. "That poor dark country was marvellously enlightened. Many were brought to Christ by his ministry; and a seed was sown in these places which to this day is not worn out.[1] Yet it is the universal testimony of his contemporaries, that Robert Bruce's own freedom and power in prayer were most striking and unusual. "He had a very majestic countenance," says one very competent witness who saw and heard him often; "and whatever he spake in public or private, yea, when he read the Word, I thought it had such force as I never dis-

---

[1] Calderwood, *History*, vi. 291f.; Bruce, *Sermons and Life* (Wod. Soc.), 125, 144.

cerned in any other man. . . . No man in his time spake with such evidence and power of the Spirit; no man had so many seals of conversion. He had a notable faculty in searching deep in the Scriptures, and of making dark mysteries plain, but especially in dealing with everyone's conscience. . . . He was both in public and private very short in prayer with others; but every sentence was like a strong bolt shot up to heaven. I have heard him say, he hath wearied when others were longsome in prayer; but being alone, he spent much time in prayer and wrestling." [1]

Or take the case of one who always regarded Robert Bruce as in a special sense his spiritual father, one whose name stands deservedly beside those of John Knox and Andrew Melville in the love and reverence of the Scottish people,— I mean Alexander Henderson. We have seen already how strongly opposed he was to the innovators who, under English influences, "discountenanced read prayers," and would have needlessly given up other usages of the old Scottish Liturgy or Book of Common Order. But none of his contemporaries, after Robert Bruce had passed away, was more eminent than he himself was in the gift and grace of prayer. All must have been struck with the evidence of this, who have studied the history of that

[1] Livingstone in *Select Biographies* (Wod. Soc.), i. 306f.

memorable Glasgow Assembly of 1638, whose proceedings Henderson guided with such singular wisdom, dignity, and success. "We ended that day," Baillie says, after telling how some difficult business had been disposed of at one of the earlier sessions of the Assembly, "with the Moderator's prayer. Among that man's other good parts, that was one,—a faculty of grave, good, and zealous prayer, according to the matter in hand; which he exercised without flagging to the last day of our meeting."[1]

Among the many striking incidents in the scene of the deposition of the prelates in the High Church of Glasgow, one of the most impressive is connected with the prayer in which Henderson, as Moderator, led the Assembly before pronouncing sentence. "It rests now," he said, "before pronouncing the sentence of this reverend and honourable Assembly, that we should call upon God, that He may be pleased to join His Divine approbation to that which we are to pronounce; that it may be seen by the world to be ratified in heaven :—

"Great Lord of the heavens and of the earth, who doest in them both what seemeth good in Thy sight: Great King and Lawgiver in Thine own Church; God eternal and glorious in Thyself, but merciful and compassionate to Thy people;

---

[1] Baillie, i. 128.

we, Thy servants and children, do again present ourselves before Thy majesty." (" *The concern of the congregation increasing,*" the old chronicler says, "as the awful part drew near, the amanuensis —evidently sharing in it—could not distinctly transcribe more of this very fervent prayer.")[1]

So much regarding the practical fruits in Scotland of the old Scottish Liturgy after it had been in regular use in the Church for nearly a century.

Again, some of the Churches on the Continent and elsewhere, which from the first have been most noted for evangelical warmth and missionary zeal, use now, and always have used, to a greater or less extent, an optional liturgy. I may refer, for example, to the Waldensian Church and to the "Unitas Fratrum" or Church of the Moravian Brethren. The same thing is true of other members of the family of Reformed Churches, well known alike for their success in missions and their soundness in the faith, such as the Dutch Reformed Church in America.[2]

I have spoken hitherto of risks and objections, and of how these may be met. In conclusion, I may point out, in a few words, several positive advantages which can hardly be gained, I think,

---

[1] *Records of the Kirk of Scotland*, 180.
[2] Compare the Author's *Grounds and Methods of Admission to Sealing Ordinances* : Edin. 1882, p. 83.

except by the plan of an optional liturgy or Book of Common Order, prepared and recommended by the authority of the Church as such.

1st. It would raise the general standard of devotional taste, if one may so speak, in public prayer.

To have some high and chaste model service, framed on the principles and in the spirit, and to a large extent in the words, of the Reformed Church in her best days, and set before ministers, elders, and people with the approval of the Church of the present, would tell gradually but steadily in this direction. It would at once aid, stimulate, and guide those entrusted with the conduct of public worship, or called upon to lead in meetings for prayer. Surely the Church owes some help of this kind to her younger ministers when first launched upon the full charge of a congregation. I have a strong persuasion that if you asked somewhat less from them, in such circumstances, in the way of extempore prayer, what you did get would be better in point of quality. It is surely the duty of our Church, while jealously guarding the freedom and elasticity of her present system, to do all that she can to remove whatever might reasonably offend the more refined and cultured among her worshippers, and hinder their edification in the common service.

2nd. An optional liturgy, rightly framed, would give the people a more direct and manifest share in the devotional part of the worship, as distinguished from the service of praise,—the congregational character of which has, as a rule, been such an admirable feature in the worship of the Presbyterian Church.

This would add perceptibly to the warmth and interest of the whole service. I do not enter here upon the question of "responses," about which a good deal may be said on both sides.[1] What I mean is that the members of the congregation should be encouraged to repeat the Lord's Prayer with the minister, and to say "Amen" at the end of all the prayers. The latter is beyond question both a Scriptural and a primitive usage.[2] It prevails to this day in several of the Reformed Churches, as, for example, in the congregations of the Waldensian Church in Italy, with great advantage to the heartiness and life of the service, as all who, like the writer, have had the privilege

---

[1] See, for instance, on the one side, Professor Lorimer, *A National Church demands a National Liturgy*, 34-8 ; and on the other, Dr. R. M. Patterson, *Presbyterian Worship* in *Presbyterian Review*, iv. 756f., 769-71 ; and as holding a middle position, Dr. Shields, *Liturgia Expurgata, or the Prayer-book as amended by the Westminster Divines*, New York, 4th ed. 39f.

[2] See above, p. 19f. ; Deut. xxvii. 15-26 ; 1 Chron. xvi. 36 ; Ps. cvi. 48 ; Neh. viii. 6 ; 1 Cor. xiv. 16. See also Ebrard's extracts from the Preface to the Liturgy of the Church of Neufchatel, *Reformirtes Kirchenbuch*, xxvii.f.

of worshipping regularly with them, even for a few weeks, must have felt.

The recitation of the "Belief" or "Apostles' Creed" on certain occasions by the whole congregation was a commendable usage of the old Scottish Church, which might well be revived where Sessions regard it as for edification. It formed a part, for instance, of the "Order of the Election of Elders and Deacons in the Church of Edinburgh," drawn up by John Knox, which was approved of by the General Assembly of 1582, and ordered to be of use in the whole Church at the ordination and admission of Elders.[1]

3rd. Such a Book of Common Order would supply what is often greatly needed—a service-book for Presbyterian worship on special occasions, at sea, in India, in the colonies, &c., where no minister is available, but where there is a strong desire for some kind of religious service, and especially for one which will remind the worshippers of home and of the Church of their fathers.

4th. Such an optional liturgy would be a practical defence of "the rights of the Christian people" in connection with the administration of Baptism and at marriage.

The nature and variety of the vows laid upon

---

[1] Dunlop, *Collection of Confessions*, ii. 636 ; Knox's Works, ii. 143, 151-54.

parents from the pulpit at the Baptism of their children sometimes constitute a serious practical abuse. A man has really a right to know distinctly beforehand what he is to be asked to assent to in such circumstances, where he has no chance of objection or reply. Then, on the other hand, the Church has to guard her own responsibility in the administration of this Sacrament as well as in that of the Lord's Supper. She has a right to see that the main points in the Scriptural and Confessional doctrine of Baptism, in its practical bearing both on the children and on the parents, shall be plainly and briefly brought before the minds of the witnessing congregation, young and old, as well as of the parents who take the vows upon themselves.

5th. Such a service-book would open to us the stores of devotional feeling and expression which lie hid in the early Christian liturgies and in those of the Reformation period.

We lose much by not studying these more than is commonly done, and seeking to catch something of their warmth, simplicity, and reverence. Why should not our ministers and people know, for instance, as well as our forefathers did in the days of Knox and Melville, that noble " Confession of Sins," which is ascribed to Œcolampadius, the friend of Zwingli, and the

Reformer of Basel? It appears in the Liturgy of the Protestant Church of Zürich, in 1525.[1] It is the second "Confession of Sins" in Calvin's "Book of Geneva"; the first in the Scottish Book of Common Order. It is used in the Waldensian Valleys, and in all the various branches of the Church of Holland, and of the Church of the Huguenots in the Old World and in the New. It stands in all the Swiss, all the French, all the Rhineland Liturgies to this day. For well-nigh four hundred years that Confession has been on the lips and in the heart of the Reformed Church all over the world. Yet we have forgotten it in Scotland since the Westminster Assembly. We have equally forgotten those Scottish Collects and other prayers of the sixteenth century of which Alexander Henderson thought so highly.

6th. Such a service-book, embodying some of these historic prayers and other ancient materials of devotion, would make our people realise, more practically than they do, the true unity of the

---

[1] See Appendix C.

The fine "General Confession" in the morning and evening service of the Church of England is taken, like much else in the Prayer-book, from Presbyterian sources. It comes from Calvin's Strassburg Service-Book of 1545, through the liturgies of Pollanus and À Lasco. See Shield's *Lit. Expurg.* 4th ed. 77f., 87-90; Daniel, *The Prayer-Book*, 8th ed. 83; Baird, *Chapter on Liturgies*, Lond. 1856, 22, 34f.

Church of Christ in what is best and highest in all ages of her history.

The voice of prayer, as well as of praise, is really one throughout all time in the Church Catholic. Prayers like that of Chrysostom, like that great Reformation Confession of Sins, never lose their power by repetition. They keep the dew of their youth through all the centuries.

We "believe in the Holy Catholic Church, the Communion of Saints." I know no better commentary on that phrase in the Apostles' Creed than the 26th chapter of the Westminster Confession of Faith, "of the Communion of Saints." But there has come to be an excess of individualism in our Church life. There is among us a great deal of—so to speak—*dormant* brotherly feeling of a really genuine kind towards each other and towards all the Churches of Christ. But it fails to find sufficient embodiment in practical ways. There is often a want of visible and practical expression of that sense of common Christian fellowship in the one Church of Christ which is in itself such a power for good. "Those long unbroken melodies of praise and prayer"[1] help us to realise and, to some extent, to express it.

The Church of England has no more exclusive right to the "Te Deum," to the "Prayer of St. Chrysostom," or to the Litany, than she has to

[1] Hitchcock, *Proceedings of Council at Philadelphia*, 74.

G

the Apostles' Creed and the Lord's Prayer. Such hymns and prayers form part of the common heritage of Christendom. They hand down to us the best thoughts and words of some of the holiest of Christ's servants, and the nearest to God in prayer and praise. Why should not our people get the good and feel the power of them, if it can be done without losing the spiritual freshness and freedom, the elasticity and simplicity which characterise our present system in good hands?

APPENDICES.

APPENDIX A.—Comp. p. 51f.

Last Prayer in which John Knox joined on his Death-bed.

THERE are few more striking and touching scenes in the records of Church history, than those connected with the last days of John Knox. Happily a full account of them has been preserved for us in the words of two eye-witnesses,—Richard Bannatyne, the faithful servant of the Reformer; and "a pious and learned man who sat with him in his sickness until his latest breath," and who, as Dr. Laing shows, was in all likelihood Mr. James Lawson, Knox's colleague and successor in St. Giles. I give the following extracts from their narratives, as illustrating Knox's use of the Apostles' Creed and of the prayers of the Book of Common Order:—

"He earnestly desired," Bannatyne says, "the Kirk—I mean the elders and deacons—that he might bid them his last good-night, as he had done before in the pulpit at the inauguration of Mr James Lawson, saying, that he would never enter that place again. Upon Monday the 17th day (of November, 1572), the Kirk came according to his desire. . . . And so with exhortation unto them all, he commendeth them to God: who, after the prayer read 'for the Sick,' as it is in the Psalm-Book, departed with tears. . . . Sunday the 23rd day—which was the first Sunday of the Fast —at afternoon, all being at the Kirk except them that waited upon him, after that he had lain a good space very quiet, as we thought, he says: 'Gif any be present, let them come and see the work of God,' for then he thought to have departed, as we judged. At what time I sent for John Johnston he bursts forth in these words: 'I have been in meditation thir two last nights of the troubled Kirk of God, the spouse of Jesus Christ, despised of the world, but precious in His sight. I have called to God for her, and have committed her to her Head, Jesus Christ. I have been fightand against Satan, who is ever ready to assault; yea, I have fochten against spiritual wickedness in heavenly things, and have prevailed. I have been in heaven and have possession; and I have tasted of these heavenly joys, where presently I am!' And thereafter said the Lord's Prayer and the Belief, with some paraphrase upon every petition and article of them; and in saying, 'Our Father which art in heaven,' he says: 'Who can pronounce so holy words?'

"After the sermon many come in to see him; and some seeing him draw his breath so shortly, asked, 'Gif he had any pain?' Whilk when he understood, he answered and said: 'I have no more pain than he that is now in heaven, and I am content, gif God so please, to lie here for seven years!' Thereafter he said oft and sundry times: 'Live in Christ, and let never flesh fear death.' His meaning was, that gif we live in Christ, no man shall fear death.

"When he would be lying, as we supposed on a sleep, then was he at his meditation, as his manifold sentences may well declare; as this, that I have before said, wherein he would often burst forth: 'Live in Christ,' and, 'Lord, grant us the right and perfect hatred of sin, as well by the document of Thy mercies as of Thy judgments.' 'Lord, grant true pastors to Thy Kirk, that purity of doctrine may be retained; and restore peace again to this commonwealth, with godly rulers and magistrates.' 'Ance, Lord, make an end of trouble!' 'Lord, I commend my spirit, soul, and body, and all, into Thine hands.' With innumerable sic like sentences.

"Monday, which was the 24th of November, he departed this life to his eternal rest. . . . Being asked by the guidman of Kinzeancleuch. 'Gif he had any pain?' said: 'It is no painful pain; but sic a pain as, I trust, shall put end to this battle.' He said also to the said Robert: 'I maun leave the care of my wife and bairns to you; to whom ye maun be a husband in my room.'

"A little after noon, he caused his wife read the 15th chapter of the First Epistle to the Corinthians, of the resurrection; to whom he said: 'Is not that a comfortable chapter?' A little after he says: 'Now, for the last, I commend my soul, spirit, and body'—

pointing upon his three fingers—'into Thine hands, O Lord.' Thereafter, about five hours, he says to his wife: 'Go, read where I cast my first anchor.' And so she read the 17th of John's Evangel; quhilk being ended, was read some of Calvin's Sermons upon the Ephesians. We, thinking that he was asleep, demanded gif he heard? Answered: 'I hear; and understand far better, I praise God.'

"About seven hours at even, we left reading, thinking he had been asleep, so he lay still till after ten hours, except that sometimes he would bid wet his mouth with a little weak ale. And half-an-hour after ten or thereby we went to our ordinar prayers, quhilk was the longer or we went to them, because we thought he had been sleepand; quhilk being ended, Dr. Preston says to him, 'Sir, heard ye the prayers?' Answered: 'I would to God that ye and all men heard them as I have heard them; and I praise God for that heavenly sound.' After the said doctor was risen up, Robert Campbell sits down before him on a stool; and suddenly thereafter he says: 'Now it is come!' for he had given a long sigh and sob. Then Richard, sitting down before him, said: 'Now, sir, the time that ye have long called to God for, to wit, an end of your battle, is come. And seeing all natural power now fails, remember upon those comfortable promises which oftentimes ye have shown to us of our Saviour Jesus Christ. And that we may understand and know that ye hear us, make us some sign.' And so he lifted up his one hand, and incontinent thereafter rendered the spirit, and slept away without any pain, the day aforesaid about eleven hours at even." [1]

The Latin narrative of Knox's last illness and death published by Smeton in 1579, and written, as there is every reason to believe, by Lawson, gives a similar account of the incident above mentioned in connection with the evening prayer. It says:—

"In the meantime evening prayers were read. Being asked if he heard them, he answered: 'I wish that you may have heard them with the same ears, and understood them with the same mind with which I heard and understood. Lord Jesus receive my spirit!'

"As there now appeared certain indications of immediate death, those who stood by requested him that he would give some certain sign that he closed his life in that eternal truth of God which he had taught, and in the steady assurance of a blessed immortality through Jesus Christ, which he had so often thirsted for. Wherefore, acquiring as it were new strength when he was just dying, he raised his hand towards heaven, and giving two sighs, his soul departed from the mortal body at eleven o'clock of the night of the 24th of November—without any motion of the feet or of any other part of his body, so that he rather seemed to fall asleep than die. Surely, whatever opprobrious things profane persons may say, in

[1] Knox's Works, vi. 637-44.

him God hath set us an example both of living and dying well."[1]

I subjoin part of the " Prayer for the Sick," which was evidently intended to be used in different parts, according to the circumstances of the sick person, and the concluding petitions of the " Evening Prayer" in the Book of Common Order, ed. 1564.

"A Prayer to be said in Visiting the Sick.

*   *   *   *   *   *

"Receive him, Lord, into Thy protection, for he hath his recourse and access to Thee alone. Make him constant and firm in Thy commandments and promises. And also pardon all his sins, both secret and those which are manifest; by the which he hath most grievously provoked Thy wrath and judgments against him; so as, in place of death,—the which both he and all we have justly merited,—Thou wilt grant unto him that blessed life, which we also attend and look for by Thy grace and mercy.

"If the time by Thee appointed be come, that he shall depart from us unto Thee, make him to feel in his conscience, O Lord, the strength and fruit of Thy grace, that thereby he may have a new taste of Thy fatherly care over him from the beginning of his life unto the very end of the same, for the love of Thy dear Son, Jesus Christ our Lord. Give him Thy

---

[1] Knox's Works, vi. 660. Comp. M'Crie, *Life of Knox*, 5th ed. ii. 221f., 227-32.

grace, that with a good heart, and full assurance of faith, he may receive to his consolation so great and excellent a treasure, to wit, the remission of his sins in Christ Jesus Thy Son, who now presenteth Himself to this poor person in distress, by virtue of Thy promises revealed unto him by Thy Word, which he hath exercised with us in Thy Church and congregation.

" Also, O Heavenly Father, vouchsafe to have pity on all other sick persons, and such as be by any other means afflicted; and also on those who as yet are ignorant of Thy truth, and appertain, nevertheless, unto Thy kingdom. Have mercy in like manner on those that suffer persecution, tormented in prisons, or otherwise troubled by the enemies of the verity for bearing testimony to the same; finally, on all the necessities of Thy people, and upon all the ruins or decays which Satan hath brought upon Thy Church.

" Grant these our requests, O our dear Father, for the love of Thy dear Son our Saviour Jesus Christ; who liveth and reigneth with Thee in the unity of the Holy Ghost, true God for evermore. So be it."[1]

A FORM OF PRAYERS TO BE USED IN PRIVATE HOUSES EVERY MORNING AND EVENING.

Evening Prayer.

*　　*　　*　　*　　*　　*

" And because Thou hast commanded us to pray one for another, we do not only make request, O Lord, for ourselves, and them that Thou hast already called

[1] Knox's Works, vi. 330f.

to the true understanding of Thy heavenly will, but for all people and nations of the world. As they know by Thy wonderful works that Thou art God over all; so may they be instructed by Thy Holy Spirit to believe in Thee their only Saviour and Redeemer. But, forasmuch as they cannot believe except they hear, nor can they hear but by preaching, and none can preach except they be sent; therefore, O Lord, raise up faithful distributors of Thy mysteries, who, setting apart all worldly respects, may both in their life and doctrine only seek Thy glory.

"Finally, forasmuch as it hath pleased Thee to make the night for man to rest in, as Thou hast ordained him the day to travel; grant, O dear Father, that we may so take our bodily rest that our souls may continually watch for the time that our Lord Jesus Christ shall appear for our deliverance out of this mortal life. And in the mean season, grant that we may fully set our minds upon Thee, love Thee, fear Thee, and rest in Thee.

"Furthermore, may our sleep be not excessive or overmuch after the desires of our flesh, but only sufficient to content our weak nature, that we may be better disposed to live in all godly conversation, to the glory of Thy holy name and profit of our brethren. So be it."[1]

---

[1] Knox's Works, vi. 352. Comp. Liturgical Services of the Reign of Queen Elizabeth (Parker Soc.), 259-63.

APPENDIX B.—SEE PP. 64-6.

SCOTTISH COLLECTS OF 1595.

THESE Collects, or "Prayers on the Psalms," are, as stated above, one hundred and forty-nine in number, the prayers on Psalm cvii. and Psalm cviii. being the same. They are all framed according to the approved liturgical rules for the construction of a Collect, with an "Invocation," "Petition," and "Conclusion," except the last ten, which are short prayers of a simpler form. Two of these are given below: "Deliver us, O Lord, from the wicked," and "Most worthy art Thou of all praises." The original text may be seen in Dr. Livingston's "Scottish Metrical Psalter of 1635," Appendix, ix-xviii. I give at the foot of the page, *verbatim et literatim*, the text of the first Collect of those selected.[1]

In the English Psalter, usually known as that of Archbishop Parker (who died in 1575), there

---

[1] "A prayer upon the fortieth Psalme :—'O Lord, that be Thy Providence gydis and governis all thingis, and that hes send to us Thy weil belovit Sonne, for to delyver us from sinne and deith be the oblatioun of His bodie on the Croce. Graunt that wee continuallie may acknawledge this Thy great and inestimabill benefite, and that wee ever haif our heartis and mouthes open to pronounce Thy praises amang all men be Thy selfsame Sonne, Jesus Christ our Saviour. So be it.'"

is a "Collecte" added after each Psalm. This—which, as Dr. Livingston observes, is "the only known precedent"—may have suggested the Scottish Prayers on the Psalms. But the prayers themselves are altogether different; the Scottish ones being, so far as I have compared the two, decidedly superior in simplicity, fervour and power of expression.

In the last will or inventory (1578) of Thomas Bassandyne, a famous Edinburgh printer, there occurs the entry: "1280 Prayers upon the Psalms, the piece 10d." These may be the Collects which we are now considering. If so, they must have been printed separately, previous to their admission into the authorised "Psalm-book." The case of Bassandyne, by the way, furnishes another illustration of the close supervision exercised by the General Assembly over everything printed in, or in connection with, their "Psalm-book" or Book of Common Order. It was reported and proved to the Assembly of 1568 that Thomas Bassandyne had published an edition of the Psalm-book with a song called "Welcome, Fortune," printed at the end, and that he had also published another book with a title which seemed to imply the king's supremacy in spiritual things; "whilk books he had printed without licence of the magistrate or revising of the Kirk. Therefore, the hail Assembly ordained the said

Thomas to call in again all the foresaid books that he has sold, and keep the rest unsold until he alter the foresaid title; and also that he delete the said song out of the end of the Psalm-book; and further, that he abstain in all time coming from printing anything without licence of the supreme magistrate and revising of sic things as pertain to religion by some of the Kirk appointed for that purpose. Attour, the Assembly appointed Mr. Alex. Arbuthnot to revise the rest of the foresaid tractate, and report to the Kirk what doctrine he finds therein."[1]

In editing this little selection of Scottish Collects, I have followed the rule on which I have acted in quoting from old writers in the preceding chapters; that is to say, I have generally modernised the spelling and punctuation, but retained the words of the original. The language of these Collects of 1595 is more distinctively Scottish than that of the prayers in the Book of Common Order. In the latter, John Knox's style may be more seen, and he was accused by his contemporaries of "knapping Southron."[2] But in these Collects there are a number of purely Scottish words, most of which I have reluctantly translated, although the nearest English equivalent is often a very inade-

---

[1] Livingston, *Scottish Met. Psalter of* 1635, p. 37; *Book of Univ. Kirk*, 100f.
[2] M'Crie, *Life of Knox*, 5th ed. ii. 277f.

quate substitute. Thus I have put "looking for," or "awaiting" in place of the fine Scots word "abidand;" "frailty" for "bruckilness," "overthrow" for "dounthring," &c. I have also occasionally made such trifling changes as to substitute "who" for "that," "heavenly" for "celestial," and "Church" for its Scottish equivalent "Kirk;" and have sometimes omitted half of a double phrase, as in the "Prayer for defence of Christ's kingdom," "destroy [and dissipate]," "devised [and addressed] against Him." Short headings have been added to indicate the nature of the prayers, and they have been grouped according to their subject-matter.

I. Prayers relating to Individual Christian Life and Experience.

1. A prayer that we may glory in Christ's Cross :—

"O Lord, who by Thy Providence dost guide and govern all things, and hast sent unto us Thy well-beloved Son to deliver us from sin and death by the oblation of His body on the Cross : Grant that we may continually acknowledge this Thine unspeakable gift, and that we may ever have our hearts and mouths open to proclaim Thy praises among all men, by the selfsame Jesus Christ our Saviour. Amen."

2. A prayer for the forgiveness of sins :—

"O pitiful Father, who art full of mercy and dost never reject the prayers of them who call upon Thee in truth: Have mercy upon us, and take away the multitude of our sins, according to the truth of Thy promises which Thou hast given us, and wherein we put our whole trust, even as we are taught by the Word of Thy Son our only Saviour. Amen."

3. Confession of sins and prayer for grace :—

"Father, most pitiful and gracious, albeit through our unthankfulness and wickedness we cease not to provoke Thee to anger against us by loosing the bridle to all our evil affections, yet notwithstanding, since it hath pleased Thee to take us into the holy covenant which Thou hast made with our fathers, we beseech Thee punish us not according to the rigour of Thy justice, but deliver us from sin and trouble, that we may give praise and thanks unto Thy holy name, through Jesus Christ our only Saviour. Amen."

4. For forgiveness and consecration to God's service :—

"Father of all mercies, who delightest not in the death of a sinner, have compassion upon us, and wash us from all our sins that we have committed against Thee since the time we first came into this world. Create in us a clean heart, and strengthen us continually with the power of Thy Holy Spirit, that we, being truly consecrated to Thy service, may set forth Thy praises, through Jesus Christ our Saviour. Amen."

5. That we may do God's will:—

"Almighty God, of whom cometh all our sufficiency, assist us by Thy Holy Spirit, that we neither think, nor say, nor do anything that is against Thy holy will. Hear our prayers. Defeat our enemies. And comfort us by the selfsame Spirit, that we may continually feel Thy fatherly favour and goodwill, which Thou showest unto Thine own children, through Jesus Christ Thy Son. Amen."

6. For the right ordering of our lives:—

"Good Lord and God Almighty, who according to Thy promises has sent unto us Thy dear Son, our King and Redeemer: Grant that we so order our lives under the obedience of Thy holy Word that we may renounce ourselves and all our carnal affections, and that we may be an occasion to all people to glorify Thy holy name throughout all the earth, and that through the self-same Jesus Christ our only Saviour. Amen."

7. For a steadfast faith and an upright life.

"Most potent King of kings and Lord of lords, whose glory is unsearchable, whose majesty is sovereign, and whose power is infinite: maintain Thy servants in quietness. And grant that we may be so settled on the certainty of Thy promises, that whatsoever thing may come upon us, we may abide firm in Thy faith, and may live uprightly and without reproach in the midst of Thy Church, which Jesus Christ Thy Son hath bought with His precious blood. Amen."

8. For quietness and thankfulness of heart.

"O eternal God and most merciful Father, who quickenest things that be dead: Of Thine infinite goodness give unto us quietness of heart, to the intent that we, not being overthrown with the heavy burdens of affliction that lie upon us, may in our consciences rejoice in Thy salvation. And grant, we beseech Thee, that we may continually addict ourselves to praise and magnify Thy most holy name, through Jesus Christ, Thy dear Son, our Redeemer. Amen."

9. For the right use of affliction.

"Good Lord, who art a just Judge and chastenest Thy children as a Father to drive them to unfeigned repentance: Grant unto us of Thine infinite goodness that the afflictions, which we justly suffer for our offences, may serve us unto the amendment of our lives; and that in the midst of them we may have a perfect feeling of Thy fatherly mercy, to the intent that, our enemies being put to shame, we may praise Thee with thanksgiving all the days of our life, through Jesus Christ, Thy Son. Amen."

10. For deliverance out of trouble.

"True and ever-living God, the only Help of all Thy poor afflicted people: Disappoint, we pray Thee, the devices of our enemies; and let all who trust in Thy promises feel Thy fatherly goodness. Despise not our prayers, but be helpful to us in the time of our troubles; that we may give Thee continual praises for delivering us out of all dangers, through Jesus Christ, Thy dear Son. Amen."

11. That we may walk uprightly in this present evil world.

"Heavenly Father, who hast adopted us to be Thy children: Grant that we, passing through this corrupt world in such integrity and cleanness that none have any just occasion to plaint of us, may in the end be participant of that blessed heritage which is prepared for Thy people in the heavens, through Jesus Christ, our only Saviour. Amen."

12. That we may follow Christ in taking up the Cross.

"Eternal God, who hast appointed Thine only Son our King and Priest, that we might be sanctified by His sacrifice of Himself upon the Cross: Grant that we may in such sort be participant of His benefits that we may renounce our own selves, and serve Him in all holiness and purity of life, and may offer up spiritual sacrifices, acceptable unto Thee, through the self-same Jesus Christ, our Lord. Amen."

13. That we may keep God's commandments.

"Most merciful God, Author of all good things, who hast given unto us Thy holy commandments, whereby we should direct our life: Imprint them in our hearts by Thy Holy Spirit. And grant that we may so renounce all our fleshly desires, and all the vanities of this world, that our whole delight may be in Thy law; that we, being always governed by Thy holy Word, may in the end attain unto that eternal salvation which Thou hast promised through Jesus Christ Thy Son. Amen."

14. For humility.

"Almighty Lord, who resistest the proud, but givest grace to the humble: Suffer not that we be lifted up in any proud opinion or conceit of ourselves in any good thing. But may we think humbly of ourselves before Thy Divine Majesty, without feigning. And may we mortify daily the deeds of the body, in such sort that in all our doings we may continually feel Thy fatherly favour, mercy, and assistance, through Jesus Christ Thy Son. Amen."

15. Against worldliness and unthankfulness of spirit.

"O God, the Creator of heaven and earth: Thou seest how the cares and business of this world do oftentimes greatly trouble and turn us from rendering to Thee that honour and obedience which are most due. Yet we beseech Thee that, forgetting all other things, we may learn aright to praise and glorify Thee all the days of our life, for the great benefits which we continually receive at Thy hands, through Jesus Christ our Lord. Amen."

16. For holiness of life.

"Almighty God, the only Deliverer of the poor and wretched, who hast delivered us from the servitude of sin and the tyranny of Satan through Thy Son Jesus Christ, the Saviour of the world: Grant that we, rightly acknowledging this Thy so great redemption, may walk safely under Thy government in all holiness of life, until we attain to the full possession of the true land of the living, where we may continually praise Thee, through the self-same Jesus Christ our Lord. Amen."

17. That we may be steadfast in God's service, and find mercy in the Day of Judgment.

"O God, the Author of all goodness, who governest the whole world by Thy marvellous wisdom: Suffer us not to be in anywise moved by the prosperous success of the ungodly; but may we the rather give ourselves wholly to Thy service, and to meditation on Thy Word; that in the end we may effectually find Thee to be our Saviour and Redeemer, when Thou shalt come to judge the world through thy well-beloved Son, Christ Jesus our Lord. Amen."

18. That we may rightly acknowledge God in His works of Creation and Providence.

"O dear Father, whose Providence reacheth over all Thy creatures in such sort that Thy marvellous wisdom is uttered through them all: Grant that we may exalt Thy glory, and sing praises and psalms to the forthsetting of the same; to the intent that, the wicked being banished from off the earth, we may rejoice in Thee, and in the end may be participant of that eternal life and felicity which are promised unto us through Jesus Christ Thy Son. Amen."

19. For light and strength in the Lord.

"Father of lights and Fountain of all goodness: Be helpful unto us in time of our affliction; and when we are in greatest danger hide not Thy face from us; yea, whatsoever thing fall unto us, strengthen our hearts, that we may have a continual esperance of all the good things which Thou hast promised to us through Jesus Christ our Lord. Amen."

II. PRAYERS FOR BLESSING IN THE USE OF THE MEANS OF GRACE.

1. For the right use of God's Word.

"Mighty God, to whom all glory and honour do justly appertain: Since it hath pleased Thee to make us understand Thy will by Thy holy Word, grant likewise that we may receive the same with all reverence, and that we may have a feeling of the force and strength thereof; that thereby we may be reformed in all holiness of life; that in the end we may enjoy the heritage promised to all them that are adopted in Thy well-beloved Son, Christ Jesus. Amen."

2. For blessing in God's House.

"O loving God, who hast promised to be nigh unto all them that call upon Thee in truth: Grant unto us now that we may so call upon Thee, in open assembly, that we may find Thy grace and fatherly favour more and more; so that, being kept in the kingdom of Thy Son Jesus Christ, we may obtain full victory over all things that are against us. Amen."

3. A prayer for the public assemblies of the Church.

"Most merciful Father, without the knowledge of Whom we can in no wise attain unto life everlasting, seeing it hath pleased Thee of Thy mercy to grant us freedom to convene ourselves together, to call upon Thy most holy name, and to hear healthsome and sound doctrine as out of Thine own mouth: Continue, we beseech Thee, this Thy goodness toward us and our posterity; and defend the cause of all who walk before Thee in innocency and cleanness of life; that we may be encouraged more and more to put our whole trust and confidence in Thee, and that through the merits of Jesus Christ, Thy dear and only Son our Saviour. Amen."

4. For blessing in Christ's kingdom on earth.

"Eternal God, the only Author of all good things, since it hath pleased Thee to receive us into the fellowship of Thy well-beloved Son our Lord Jesus Christ: Suffer us not in any wise to be overcome of our enemies; but grant that, His kingdom being established in the midst of us, we may triumphantly sing and magnify His praises both now and evermore. Amen."

5. For the defence of Christ's kingdom, and for growth in grace.

"Almighty God and heavenly Father, who hast given unto us Thy dear Son to be our Lord and King: We beseech Thee that Thou wouldst destroy by Thy marvellous wisdom all enterprises devised against Him throughout the whole world. And make us so to profit and grow in His holy law and doctrine, that in all fear and reverence we may serve Thee; that in the end we may attain to that endless joy which we hope to receive through the same Jesus Christ Thy Son. Amen."

6. For the spirit of prayer and the fruit thereof.

"Eternal God, who makest all things to turn to the best for them that love Thee, and who preservest all those who give themselves into Thy keeping: Grant us, of Thy bountiful grace, that we may continually call upon Thee with our whole hearts; that we, being delivered from all dangers, may in the end enjoy that salvation which is purchased for us by Jesus Christ, Thine only Son, our Saviour. Amen."

7. For blessing in the Church through the Word and Sacraments.

"O Eternal God, the only Founder and Keeper of Thy Church: Grant that we, being placed under the government of Jesus Christ, the only Chief and Head thereof, may be comforted by Thy most holy Word, and strengthened and confirmed by Thy Sacraments;

to the intent that we all, with one heart and mouth, may glorify Thee, and edify one another in holiness of life and godly conversation through the selfsame Jesus Christ our Lord. Amen."

8. A prayer after the Communion.

"O loving Father, who by Thine oath hast promised unto us a Saviour, Jesus Christ Thy Son: Thou hast not deceived us, but hast indeed given Him unto us, as Thy Word hath declared; and by Thy Sacraments Thou hast confirmed it unto us this day; yea, He hath further promised that He will abide with us even unto the end of the world. Therefore, dear Father, we beseech Thee that Thou wilt bless us in all our ways, govern us, and replenish us with joy. Let thy Crown and Kingdom abide above us; and preserve us in peace through the same Jesus Christ Thy Son. Amen."

9. For peace and good-will among Christ's people.

"Gracious Lord, who art not a God of confusion, but the God of concord and of peace: Join our hearts and affections in such sort together that we may walk as brethren in Thy House, in brotherly kindness and love, and as members of the Body of Christ. Let the grace of Thy Holy Spirit enkindle us, and the dew of Thy blessing continually fall upon us, that we may together in the end obtain life eternal through the same Jesus Christ our Lord. Amen."

III. Prayers for the Church.

1. That Christ's kingdom may prosper and we therein.

"Almighty God, the Help and Defence of all them that fear Thee: Grant that we may ever live under the safeguard of Thy well-beloved Son Jesus Christ. Grant also that His kingdom may prosper, and be advanced daily more and more; and that we, being settled upon Thy promises, may render unto Thee the sacrifices of praise and thanksgiving, both now and evermore. Amen."

2. That the Church and truth of God may be upheld in purity.

"Most puissant God of hosts, who upholdest and keepest all them that trust in Thee: Bend forth Thine invincible force against the enemies of Thy truth. Make feeble the strength of the proud. Turn our troubles into prosperity. And grant that in the midst of our assemblies the praise of Thy holy name may so be celebrate as shall be most in accordance with Thy Word, declared unto us by Thy Son Jesus Christ our Lord. Amen."

3. For the defence and purity of the Church.

"O mighty King and Lord, the Rock and Fortress of all them who put their trust in Thee: Undo the force and break down the pride of those who afflict Thy Church. Suffer not the simple to be overthrown; but stablish them as Mount Zion, that they may abide in the New Jerusalem, which is Christ's Church. Suffer us not to shake hands with unrighteousness; but let peace be upon Israel, even upon all them who walk not after the flesh but after the Spirit, through the selfsame Jesus Christ our Lord. Amen."

4. That the Church of God may be gathered into one and fed from His Word.

"O Lord, marvellous are Thy might and power, whereby Thou castest down the proud, and liftest up such as be humble and meek: We beseech Thee of Thy great mercy to restore and rebuild Thy Church, which was founded by Thee only. Gather together Thy scattered sheep. As Thou feedest all creatures with temporal food and pasturage, make us to feel inwardly the effect of Thy holy Word: and grant that we, following Thy will declared therein, may in the end enjoy the heritage prepared for Thy people in Christ Jesus. Amen."

5. For the Church under the Cross.

"Eternal Father and God of all comfort, who, for satisfaction of our sins, didst cast down Thine only Son to extreme anguish and dolour, and hast ordained Thy Church to pass by the same way of affliction: We beseech Thee most fervently that, forasmuch as we are destitute of all help of men, we the more be assured of Thy mercy and goodness, that we may praise the same before all creatures both now and evermore. Amen."

6. For succour to Christ's flock in perplexities.

"Lord God, who canst put in order things confused and out of order: Arise and stretch forth Thine arm to cast down the proudness of such as lift up themselves against Thee and persecute Thy little flock; to the intent that, all resistance trodden down, Thou mayest be acknowledged as the Saviour and Protector of all them that trust in Thee through Jesus Christ our Lord. Amen."

7. That the Church may be freed from enemies and follow Christ only.

"Almighty God, who of Thy goodness hast placed us in the sheepfold of Thy Son Jesus Christ, that we should be governed by Him as the only Shepherd and Bishop of our souls: Turn not away thy face from us; but look down from heaven and behold how these our enemies seek our destruction. Frustrate their fury, we beseech Thee; and defend us from all evils, that we may render Thee perpetual praises through the selfsame Jesus Christ our Lord. Amen."

8. For deliverance to the Church in time of peril.

"O Lord, the Ruler and Governor of the whole world, teach us to praise Thy holy name perpetually. Preserve Thy poor Church from destruction. Repress the pride and boldness of her adversaries. Bring down the despisers of Thy blessed Word; to the intent that, when the ungodly are casten down and the godly exalted, all men may give unto Thee due honour, praise, and glory through Jesus Christ our Lord. Amen."

9. *That we may remember all the way by which God hath led His Church.*

"Eternal God, the only Refuge of comfortless creatures: Hear now our prayers and petitions, and turn not away Thy mercy from us. Give us grace so to acknowledge Thy marvellous works, which Thou hast shown to Thy people in times past, that we may be daily more and more confirmed in the assurance of Thy goodness, by the which Thou hast freely elected and adopted us in Thy well-beloved Son Jesus Christ. Amen."

10. *For the spread of the Gospel, and the good of the Catholic Church.*

"O Lord God, the only Founder of Thy Church: Increase daily the number of the faithful by the preaching of Thy holy Evangel. May the darkness of ignorance be chased out of the world, and Thy name be known over all. May all men resort out of all places to render themselves under the obedience of Thy Word; and may they reverence Thee with their whole hearts, through Jesus Christ our Lord. Amen."

11. *For the spread of the Gospel among all nations.*

"Almighty and everlasting God, who, after a marvellous manner, hast wrought the redemption of man in sending Thine only Son to fulfil the promises made unto our fathers: Open up more and more the knowledge of that salvation; that in all parts of the earth Thy truth and puissance may be made known; to the intent that all nations may praise, honour, and glorify Thee through Thy selfsame Son, Jesus Christ our Saviour. Amen."

IV. PRAYERS FOR THE NATION AND ITS RULERS.

1. For deliverance in time of national danger.

"O Lord God, King of kings, who holdest all nations under Thy subjection: Deliver us out of the danger of them who seek our wrack and destruction; to the intent that all men may know the care and love which Thou hast of Thy heritage; that we may sing psalms unto Thee through Jesus Christ our Lord. Amen."

2. For our rulers and judges.

"Eternal God, by whom kings rule, and princes ordain justice: May it please Thee so to enlighten the hearts of all judges and magistrates whom Thou hast given us, that, without exception of persons, they may uphold the righteous, and punish the wicked; to the intent that, under their protection, we may lead a quiet and peaceable life, according to the precepts given us by Jesus Christ Thy Son, our only Saviour. Amen."

V. PRAYERS BEARING ON A CHRISTIAN'S RELATIONS TO OTHERS.

1. That we may confess Christ before men.

"O loving and merciful Father, who never leavest them that put their trust in Thee, and who sendest fatherly chastening on Thy children for their own health: Grant that we may be built as lively stones upon Jesus Christ, the true and only Foundation of Thy Church; that, forasmuch as He was rejected and dispraised of men, we may acknowledge Him always for our King and Saviour; that we may enjoy the fruit of Thy mercy and goodness for evermore, through the same Jesus Christ our Lord."

2. That we may remember the poor.

"Most loving Father, without whose blessing we are altogether poor and miserable: Imprint Thy holy Word on all our hearts, in such sort that our whole delight may be to serve Thee in all fear and reverence. Grant that we may be so merciful towards our poor neighbours, that we also may have a sure feeling of Thy mercy and goodness when Thou shalt come to judge the world in Him whom Thou hast ordained to be our Lord and Sovereign, Jesus Christ. Amen."

3. For help in the troubles of this world.

"Eternal Father, who art the only true God and the Deliverer of poor captives and prisoners: We beseech Thee of Thy plentiful bounty to relieve us from the bondage of our adversaries; that we, passing through the miseries and calamities of this troublesome world, may in the end enjoy the fruit of our faith, which is the salvation of our souls, bought by the blood of Thy dear Son Christ Jesus. Amen."

4. That we may be kept from evil company.

"O loving Father, unto whom all the inward secrets

of our hearts are known : Grant that we may so walk before Thee in uprightness of conscience, that we keep no company with mockers and contemners of Thy holy Word. But may we be so circumcised in heart and mind that, renouncing all worldly friendship, we may never wander from the right way which Thou hast shown us in the Evangel of Jesus Christ Thy Son, our Saviour. Amen."

5. For deliverance from the wicked.

"Deliver us, O Lord, from the wicked and the ungodly, who in their hearts devise mischief, and delight in strife and contention. Let us not fall into their snares, nor suffer them to handle us at their will. Hear the voice of our complaint; for Thou art our God. Take the defence of our cause in Thy hand, that we may with all our hearts render unto Thee praises and thanks through Jesus Christ our Lord. Amen."

6. That God's will may be done by us and ours.

"Almighty and eternal God, who by Thy providence dost conduct and govern all creatures in this world : Suffer us not to enterprise anything but that which is according to Thy will; that we, altogether discontented with ourselves, may wholly depend upon Thy blessing; and that our only care may be that Thou mayest be glorified in us and our posterity through Jesus Christ Thy Son. Amen."

7. That God would prosper us in our affairs.

"O heavenly Father, the Creator of heaven and earth, in whom our help is : Suffer not our afflictions so to overcome us that we cast off our confidence in Thee. But do Thou guide and prosper all our enterprises, and give a happy end and issue to all our businesses, so that we may be the more assured that we are of the number of them whom Thou hast chosen unto salvation through Jesus Christ Thy Son. Amen."

8. For family blessings.

"Gracious Lord, who art the Well-spring of all felicity, grant that we may always fear Thee, and walk in Thy ways. Bless us, and all ours, that it may be well with us and all who appertain to us. May we see many generations and children of faith. May we see peace upon Israel. And so may we glorify Thee all the days of our lives, through Jesus Christ Thy Son. Amen."

9. A prayer for all men that they may be saved.

"O good Lord, who willest all people to be saved and to come to the knowledge of Thy truth: Show forth Thy power and excellent Majesty unto the whole world, that every one may sing Thy praises and show forth Thy salvation, which Thou hast promised to all them that give themselves to Thee and to Thy service; that Thou mayest be praised in all Thy creatures, through Jesus Christ Thy Son. Amen."

VI. THANKSGIVING AND PRAISE TO GOD.

"Most worthy art Thou, O good and gracious God, of all praises, even for Thine own sake. Thou art the

Most High and Holy One, and by Thee only are we made holy. We praise Thee for our glorious redemption, purchased for us in Thy dearly beloved Son, Christ Jesus. Give us, we pray Thee, Thy Holy Spirit to govern us. And grant that all things which have breath may praise Thee, who art the true life of all creatures, through the same Jesus Christ, our Lord, who reigneth with Thee and with the Holy Ghost, One God, for ever and ever. Amen."

APPENDIX C.—See pp. 79 f.

The Reformation Confession of Sins, 1525.

"Heavenly Father, merciful and everlasting God, we acknowledge and confess before Thy Divine Majesty that we are poor miserable sinners, conceived and born in sin and corruption. We are prone to all evil. We are unable, without Thee, to do any good. And we daily, and in many ways, transgress Thy holy commandments. Thereby we provoke Thine anger against us, and purchase to ourselves, by Thy just judgment, death and ruin.

"But, O Lord, it repenteth and grieveth us that we have so displeased Thee. We condemn ourselves and our misdoings, and pray that Thy grace may bring help to our distress and misery.

"Be pleased, therefore, to have mercy upon us, O most gracious God and Father. Forgive us all our sins, through the holy sufferings of Thy dear Son, Jesus Christ our Lord. Take away our sins; and grant us the daily increase of the gifts of Thy Holy Spirit, that we, acknowledging from the bottom of our hearts our own unrighteousness, may truly repent us of the same; that sin may be destroyed in us; and that we may bring forth the fruits of righteousness and a pure life, well-pleasing unto Thee, through Jesus Christ. Amen."

I translate from Ebrard's German text of 1525, but follow in one or two cases the readings of Knox and Calvin's Book of Geneva (1554-56), and lean to its phrases so far as consistent with faithfulness to the original. I give the German below, and give also one specimen from the many liturgies of Churches of the French tongue in which this ancient confession is still in constant use.

After "bring forth such fruits as may be agreeable to Thy blessed will," the Book of Geneva, and the Scottish Book of Common Order (1564) add :—

"Not for the worthiness thereof, but for the merits of Thy dearly beloved Son, Jesus Christ our only Saviour, whom Thou hast already given an oblation and offering for our sins, and for whose sake we are certainly persuaded that Thou wilt deny us nothing that we shall ask in His name according to Thy will. For Thy Spirit doth assure our consciences that Thou art our merciful Father, and so lovest us Thy children through Him, that nothing is able to remove Thy heavenly grace and favour from us. To Thee, therefore, O Father, with the Son and the Holy Ghost, be all honour and glory, world without end. So be it."[1]

This Confession of Sins—"Die offne Schuld," as it is called in German-speaking Reformed Churches—occurs in the French Liturgy which was published by Calvin at Geneva, in 1541, but which had been drawn up by him previously, and had been used by the Protestant pastors of Geneva for several years before it was printed. Calvin's Service-Book, republished in Latin in 1545, was the chief source from which this Confession passed rapidly into use in the Reformed Church Catholic, and even in several of the Lutheran Churches.[2] It appears in English, among other prayers, at the end of an edition of Sternhold and Hopkins' Psalms, in 1566, under the title of "A Confession for all Estates and Times." It has been sometimes erroneously ascribed to Beza, who used it in a striking scene at the Colloquy of Poissy, in 1561.[3]

[1] Knox's Works, iv. 181f.; Book of Common Order (Sprott and Leishman), 80.

[2] It is used, for example, in the Liturgy of the National Church of Württemberg as the first Confession of Sins for Days of Fasting, being taken from the Service-Book of the Church of the Palatinate.—"Kirchenbuch für die Evang. Kirche in Württemberg," Stuttgart, 1843, 256f.

[3] Ebrard, *Reformirtes Kirchenbuch*, xxvi. Baird, *Chap. on*

The "General Confession" in the Anglican Communion Service, which appears in the first Prayer-Book of Edward VI. (1549), is closely akin to the Reformation Confession of Sins, especially in the form in which it appears in the document known as "Hermann's Consultation," which was compiled by Bucer and Melanchthon, at the request of Hermann, the Protestant Elector and Archbishop of Cologne.[1] The "General Confession" of the morning and evening services in the English Prayer-Book is taken, as stated above, more directly from the Liturgy drawn up by Calvin in 1543 for the Church at Strassburg, whose minister he had been during his temporary banishment from Geneva, 1538-41.

Die offne Schuld, 1525.

"Himmlischer Vater, ewiger und barmherziger Gott, wir erkennen und bekennen, vor deiner göttlichen

---

Liturgies, 34f. 77-79. Sprott and Leishman, *Book of Common Order*, 240. Liturgical Services of reign of Queen Elizabeth (Parker Soc.), p. 265.

[1] This "Consultation of us, Hermann," was to devise "by what means a Christian Reformation, and founded on God's Word, of doctrine, administration of the Divine Sacraments, of ceremonies, and the whole cure of souls, and other ecclesiastical ministries, may be begun among men committed to our pastoral charge." It first appeared in German in 1543, and in Latin in 1545. An English edition was published in 1547, and a second in the following year.—Shields, *Lit. Expurg*, 4th ed., 79f.; Daniel, *The Prayerbook*, 8th ed., 318.

Majestät, dass wir arme, elende Sünder sind, empfangen und geboren in der Verderbniss, geneigt zu allem Bösen, untüchtig ohne Dich zum Guten, und dass wir deine heiligen Gebote täglich und mannigfaltig übertreten ; dadurch wir deinen Zorn wider uns reizen und nach deinem gerechten Urtheil auf uns laden den Tod und das Verderben.

"Aber, O Herr, wir tragen Reu' und Leid dass wir Dich erzürnet haben, und verklagen uns und unsre Sünden, und begehren dass deine Gnade zu Hülfe komme unserm Elend und Jammer.

"Wollest Dich derhalben über uns erbarmen, O allergütigster Gott und Vater, und uns verzeihen alle unsere Sünden, durch das heilige Leiden deines lieben Sohnes, unseres Herrn Jesu Christi. Vergieb uns unsere Sünden, und verleihe und mehre in uns täglich die Gaben deines Heiligen Geistes, dass wir unsere Ungerechtigkeit von ganzem Herzen erkennen, und einen aufrichtigen Schmerz in uns empfinden, der die Sünde in uns zerstöre, und Früchte bringe der Unschuld und Gerechtigkeit, die Dir angenehm seien um Jesus Christi willen. Amen."[1]

La Confession des Péchés.

According to the present Liturgy of the French Reformed Church, at morning service, after an introductory sentence of prayer, a psalm or hymn is sung. Then the Ten Commandments are read. Thereafter the minister proceeds as follows :—

[1] Ebrard, *Reformirtes Kirchenbuch*, 2f.

"Maintenant que nous avons lu la loi qui condamne nos iniquités, mes frères, que chacun de nous se présente devant le Seigneur, pour Lui faire une humble confession de ses péchés en suivant du cœur ces paroles :

"Seigneur Dieu, Père Eternal et Tout-puissant, nous reconnaissons et nous confessons, devant Ta sainte Majesté, que nous sommes de pauvres pécheurs, nés dans la corruption,[1] enclins au mal, incapables par nous-mêmes de faire le bien,[1] et qui transgressons tous les jours et en plusieurs manières Tes saintes commandements ; ce qui fait que nous attirons sur nous, par Ton juste jugement, la condamnation et la mort.

"Mais, Seigneur, nous avons une vive douleur[2] de T'avoir offensé. Nous nous condamnons, nous et nos vices, avec une sérieuse repentance, recourant humblement à Ta grâce et Te suppliant de subvenir a notre misère.[2]

"Veuille donc avoir pitié de nous, Dieu très-bon, Père de miséricorde, et nous pardonner nos péchés, à cause de Ton Fils Jésus Christ notre Sauveur. Accorde-nous aussi et nous augmente continuellement les grâces de Ton Saint Esprit, afin que, reconnaissant de plus en plus nos fautes, et en étant vivement touchés, nous y renoncions de tout notre cœur, et que

---

[1] The Waldensian Liturgy keeps the original readings : "concus et nés dans le péché et dans la corruption" ; "incapables . . . d'aucun bien."

[2] Wald. : "un grand déplaisir, . . . une vraie repentance, désirant que Ta grace subvienne à notre misère."

nous portions des fruits de sainteté et de justice, qui Te soient agréables par Jésus Christ notre Seigneur. Amen."[1]

[1] La Liturgie ou l'Ordre du Service Divine selon l'usage des Églises Réformées de France : Paris, 1859, 7f. (ed. Frossard). Compare the very beautiful liturgy drawn up by M. Bersier, and used in his church in Paris, which is largely taken from the most ancient service-books of the French Reformed Church,— "Liturgie à l'Usage des Églises Reformées," Paris, ed. 1881, 39, 238, 251.

BY THE SAME AUTHOR.

Fcap. 8vo, cloth, price 1s.

GROUNDS AND METHODS

OF

ADMISSION TO SEALING ORDINANCES;

OR,

WHO SHOULD BE RECEIVED TO THE LORD'S TABLE?
WHOSE CHILDREN SHOULD BE BAPTISED?
HOW SHOULD WE RECEIVE YOUNG COMMUNICANTS?

OPINIONS OF THE PRESS.

"Very valuable. A judicious and scholarly discussion of the grounds and modes of admission to Baptism and the Lord's Supper. . . . We shall be surprised if this short treatise does not gain a wide circulation, for it deals with matters which must engage the anxious attention of intelligent pastors and elders everywhere."—*The Outlook (English Presbyterian).*

"Presbyterian ministers and elders will find this sensible little treatise to be of great use in guiding them in the practical administration of discipline."—*The Scotsman.*

"We commend the work as containing much thoughtful matter, new on this side of the Border."—*Ecclesiastical Gazette (Church of England).*

"Evidently the production of an able and well-instructed theologian. Cannot fail to be interesting to all members of the Church, but specially entitled to the attention of young ministers."—*Belfast Witness.*

"A thoughtful contribution on a most important subject, and all the more welcome because it is Catholic in its scope, and Christian and brotherly in its spirit,—the latter characteristic being specially manifest in its references to Plymouthism."—*Perthshire Advertiser.*

"Mr. Bannerman has compressed into this small volume the fruit of much reading and ripe scholarship. It will prove eminently helpful to clergymen in the performance of what must often be to them a difficult and perplexing duty."—*People's Journal.*

EDINBURGH: ANDREW ELLIOT, 17 PRINCES STREET.

www.ingramcontent.com/pod-product-compliance
Lightning Source LLC
Chambersburg PA
CBHW030403170426
43202CB00010B/1463